CASSATT

CASSATT

Alison Effeny

PORTLAND HOUSE
NEW YORK

For my Parents, of course.

This 1991 edition published by Portland House
distributed by Outlet Book Company Inc.
a Random House Company
225 Park Avenue South
New York, New York 10003

Printed and bound in Hong Kong

ISBN 0-517-05377-2

INTRODUCTION

When the sixty-eight-year-old Mary Cassatt was visited by her first biographer, Achille Segard, in 1912, she told him that when she announced her intention to pursue a career as a professional artist, her father's reaction was to declare: 'I would almost rather see you dead.' Successful, but embittered by what she saw as the failure of her country fully to appreciate her work, the artist looked back on her life as a struggle to overcome the barriers of parochialism and paternalistic authoritarianism, both at home in the United States and in the European art world to which she escaped. These barriers had certainly existed, but they had been successfully surmounted by Cassatt and other women of her generation, and her nationality and domestic circumstances were in fact to be the source and focus of her creative activity, conditioning the character of her vision and practice: a fusion of pragmatic detachment and emotional idealism. It was also to the emergent fine arts institutions of the United States that she made her most influential cultural contributions.

Mary Stevenson Cassatt was born on 22nd May 1844, into circumstances which, despite appearances, were unusually suited to the fostering of her pioneering career in the history of American art. Her father, a moderately successful banker with Huguenot ancestors, had a taste for travel and sufficient wealth to finance family trips to Europe, while her mother ensured that the children benefited from her own French education. In 1850, Robert Simpson Cassatt and Katherine Kelso Cassatt took their family – Lydia, Alexander, Robert, Mary and Joseph (referred to by his middle name, Gardner) – on an extended tour of Europe. Ostensibly, this was so that their middle son, Robbie, could receive sophisticated medical care, while Alexander went to German technical schools in Heidelberg and Darmstadt. However, a long period was also spent in Paris, during which time Mary and her siblings studied French and other languages and experienced the cultural excitements of the 1855 Exposition Universelle and the Salon, the annual showcase for the artistic establishment. Here could be seen the works of Delacroix and Ingres, and, in the *Pavillon du Réalisme*, the independent solo exhibition of Gustave Courbet, later one of Cassatt's heroes. While the eleven-year-old girl could not have appreciated the nature of the debates then raging in French artistic circles between the advocates of line and colour, led by the painters Ingres and Delacroix respectively, it must have been clear that art could be at the centre of public attention. In 1855, however, the death of Robbie at Darmstadt caused the Cassatts to return to a very different cultural setting.

In 1879, the novelist Henry James wrote: 'The soil of American perception is a poor little barren deposit.' There were few public museums and galleries in the United States until the 1870s, and young artists in America were denied first-hand exposure to masterpieces of the Western art tradition and to the innovations of their European contemporaries. To some extent the lack of a well-defined American cultural identity encouraged an individualist attitude, but at the same time it forced artists and their teachers to find a yardstick, and validation, in European systems of teaching and exhibiting.

By the time of Cassatt's sixteenth birthday she had decided on a career in art, and she was allowed to enrol as a student in the drawing classes of the Pennsylvania Academy of the Fine Arts in Philadelphia, where the family had their town residence. She was fortunate in that Philadelphia was, by 1860, the second largest city of the United States, and a thriving financial and cultural centre. Large crowds were attracted to the Academy's annual exhibitions, which included modern European art – especially French – as well as old master paintings. In 1864, Rosa Bonheur's *The Horse Fair* came to the supplementary Central Fair: this work by a highly regarded woman artist was one of the most celebrated paintings of the nineteenth century, and her success must have been an encouragement to the ambitious Cassatt. The work of her future teacher, French Academician Jean Léon Gérôme, also appeared at the exhibitions of 1860, 1861 and 1862 and was particularly admired. All these events may have spurred Cassatt in her decision to leave for Paris as soon as possible.

The Pennsylvania Academy was relatively progressive in its attitudes to women, who by 1860 constituted 30 per cent of the student body, and had opened all but the nude life-drawing class to them. The director of its curriculum, John Sartain, closely followed the teaching system of the École des Beaux-Arts in Paris, which demanded several years of copying from engravings, paintings and classical statuary before allowing its students to attempt painting. (Sartain based his own career on fine engraved reproductions of famous paintings.) The students also had lectures in anatomy from professors at the medical school. However, Cassatt felt frustrated by this regimen and followed only two years of the prescribed course before embarking on painting independently. Perversely, it was to be in the company of the Impressionists that she perfected her draughtsmanship, despite their reputation for subordinating drawing to direct painterly effects.

While at the Academy, Cassatt made the acquaintance of several other students who saw European training as essential to their artistic formation. Thomas Eakins, who was to return to the United States as a successful teacher, and Howard Roberts, a sculptor and later an American Academician, were among these. At the same time, she enjoyed the company of young people of her own wealthy background and interests, and the Academy fostered a lively social life. (See above, Cassatt stands at the right.) Her closest friend at the Academy was Eliza Haldeman, whose letters home recorded their progress in instruction: 'We keep pretty nearly together. She generally

Photograph of Mary Cassatt, Eliza Haldeman, Inez Lewis and Rebecca Welsh making a plastercast of the hand of Dr Edward A. Smith at the Pennsylvania Academy in 1862.

getting the shading better and I the form, she the "ensemble" and I the "minutia" but I am trying hard to get ahead.' Cassatt's later concentration on composition and light effects are found in embryo here.

Despite the reported opposition of her father, in late 1865 Cassatt embarked for Paris with Haldeman, as soon as travel restrictions were lifted, six months after the end of the American Civil War. There they soon discovered that the French had a more conservative attitude to female instruction than the Pennsylvania Academy, and they were denied entry to the classes at the École des Beaux-Arts. Nevertheless, both Cassatt and Haldeman were able to enrol in the ladies class run by Charles Chaplin, an Academician, and also received private instruction from Gérôme. Cassatt's lifelong attitude to training was formed at this time: she could see that the established institutions only promoted their own ideals, rather than allowing their students to develop their individual expressive power. She later told Segard that 'the instruction of the museums was sufficient' and, indeed, she and Haldeman immediately acquired the licences which enabled them to copy masterpieces in the Louvre. The reputedly misogynist Edgar Degas later depicted Cassatt in the Louvre in a series of pastels and prints which show her not merely as a fashionable female silhouette but as a serious artist intent on the lessons of the past (see p. 8).

The educational disappointments of her first year in Paris led Cassatt to turn to influences other than those of the official Salon. Early in 1867 she moved with Haldeman to the artists' colony at Courances in the Forest of Fontainebleau, where she saw the working methods of the Barbizon school, whose landscapes and peasant subjects were particularly popular with American buyers. From there they moved to another village, Ecouen, ten miles north of Paris, where they concentrated on genre painting – depicting scenes of everyday life – under its established masters Pierre Edouard Frère and Paul Soyer. Ever-practical, Cassatt may have seen this as the fastest means to win professional acceptance and sales at home, and it also reflects her sympathy for modern subjects rather than the allegorical or historical themes of the academies. Haldeman's letters leave us in no doubt of her friend's strength of purpose: 'Mary wants to be remembered to you, she laughed when I told you her message and said she wanted to paint *better* than the old masters. Her Mother wants her to be a portrait painter as she has a talent for likenesses and thinks she is very ambitious to want to paint pictures . . . I think she has a great deal of talent and industry' (15th May 1867).

'Pictures' for Cassatt always meant the representation of contemporary reality. Her mother's expectations were indicative of the limitations which had been placed on the repertoire of women with artistic ambitions in the nineteenth century. Portraiture and decorous water-colours of flowers and domestic scenes were considered suitable, but, even then, women were considered to be formed more for the inspiration of art than for its creation. Throughout her life, Cassatt resisted the attractions of a secure career in portraiture: she brought to her pictures of women a psychological presence which raised them above the level of prettified objects. As she later wrote to an American patron, Mrs Potter Palmer, she was determined 'that women should be someone and not something'.

In 1868, both Cassatt and Haldeman had their first pictures accepted by the Salon: *A Mandolin Player* by Cassatt and *A Peasant Woman* by Haldeman both demonstrated the influence of the Ecouen school. The support of Cassatt's family back in Pennsylvania was, however, undercut by patronizing sarcasm, as in this letter from Alexander to his fiancée, Lois: 'She is in high spirits as

Edgar Degas, Mary Cassatt at the Louvre: The Etruscan Gallery (Third State), *c. 1879, The Metropolitan Museum of Art, New York.*

her picture has been accepted for the annual exhibition in Paris . . . and not only has it been accepted but it has been hung on the 'line' . . . Mary's art name is 'Mary Stevenson' under which name I suppose she expects to become famous, poor child.' To be hung 'on the line' means to be exhibited at eye-level – an important advantage on the crowded Salon walls.

Cassatt may have used her middle name, 'Stevenson', to draw attention to herself as an American among so many French exhibitors, and her picture won some gratifying praise 'for its vigour of treatment and fine qualities of colour' from a *New York Times* critic. This notice mentioned her tutelage under Gérôme, although in fact *A Mandolin Player* owes more to the influence of a painter who had rejected academic standards, Thomas Couture. His teaching attracted numerous American art students to the village of Villiers-le-Bel near Ecouen, and Cassatt returned there periodically during her first years in Europe. It may have been an echo of Couture's attractive colours, tonal contrasts and free brushwork which later attracted Cassatt to the work of his pupil, Édouard Manet.

Eliza Haldeman returned to America in 1868, and abandoned her art studies for a more conventional life of marriage. Cassatt, however, remained in France, and spent the next summer on a sketching tour of the Alps with a friend, a Miss Gordon. This trip produced Cassatt's second successful entry to the Paris Salon, in 1870 – *A Peasant Woman of Fobello* (now lost) – and she could already relish her identity as an officially recognized painter: ' . . . we went to Aix-les-Bains a very fashionable watering place entirely too gay for two poor painters, at least for one, for although my friend calls herself a painter she is only an amateur and you must know we professionals despise amateurs . . . ' (1st August 1869). She continued her programme of self-instruction with a visit to Rome in the summer of 1870, but that autumn the outbreak of the Franco-Prussian War forced her to return to the United States and seemed to mark an abrupt end to her ambitions.

At home, she at first attempted to continue her work, renting a studio and placing her pictures for sale in various galleries in Philadelphia and New York. However, when the family moved to Hollidaysburg, near Altoona, where Alexander was following an increasingly successful career with the Pennsylvania Railroad, she could no longer find the materials or models she needed, and her existing paintings failed to sell. Her parents insisted that her career pay for itself and, without funds or any means of generating them, she had to close the studio. As a crowning disappointment, the paintings she had taken to Chicago for sale were destroyed in that city's worst fire, in October 1871. As a result, very little of Cassatt's earliest work now remains, apart from the unfinished *Portrait of Mrs Currey*, the Cassatt's Black housekeeper, which shows a developing interest in the working woman as a subject.

On her return to Philadelphia, Cassatt had resumed acquaintance with many of her student friends, in particular with Emily Sartain, the daughter of John Sartain and, at thirty, a successful engraver. Emily was later to have her own distinguished career in art education in the United States, but in 1871 she too wanted to go to Europe to train as a painter. Cassatt complained to Emily about the aesthetic deprivation from which she suffered, and she was later to state that art education in America would be nothing until it established funds with which to send students to Europe. Both were overjoyed when Cassatt was given a commission by the Bishop of Pittsburgh to copy two works in Parma by the sixteenth-century artist Correggio. This gave Cassatt both the money and the excuse to travel once again to Italy, in

Antonio Correggio, Assumption of the Virgin, *1524–30, fresco on the cupola of Parma Cathedral.*

December 1871, this time accompanied by Sartain.

Cassatt does not appear to have completed her commission, although we know that she did copy Correggio's *Coronation of the Virgin*. American students rarely came to Parma, and Cassatt's nationality, facility with languages and evident talent caused her to be fêted in its smaller artistic and social circles. The two women received every form of practical help from the teachers at the local academy, who gave them studio space and instruction on request. In particular, the head of the School of Engraving at the Accademia, Carlo Raimondi, became a close associate of Cassatt, and through him she was able to extend her network of artistic contacts. However, whatever her later interests, at this stage in her career she concentrated on her painting and seems not to have learned anything of printmaking techniques from Raimondi.

The galleries of Parma provided many Renaissance masters to study, and she admired in particular the work of Parmigianino as well as Correggio. Her future choice and skill in painting small children may have been influenced by these artists' frescoes seen in Parma's churches, which represent children with grace and energy. Her work would also later demonstrate the lasting appeal of classical compositional systems, and in particular of the Madonna and Child subject, which can be traced back to her stay in Parma. As late as 1913 she talked of revisiting the city to study Parmigianino and his influence over other old masters whom she admired.

This period produced further paintings for the Paris Salon, though ones very different in style from her earlier entries. She had found more exotic subject-matter in Italy, both festive contemporary scenes and dramatically posed classical figures, and her work known to come from Parma includes *Two Women Throwing Flowers During Carnival* (which probably corresponds to the painting titled *At the Carnival* accepted for the 1872 Salon) and *Bacchante*. This latter marks her only experiment with the classical staples of the academies. Both these paintings demonstrate her already developing interest in the portrayal of female characters in active poses, engaging with their surroundings and projecting a strong physical presence.

Meanwhile, Emily Sartain had moved on to Paris, to further her training in the atelier of the Salon painter Evariste Luminais, but the two women kept in touch by writing. Cassatt remained in Parma until the autumn of 1872, when she moved on to Spain. Her first pictures there were copies made in the Prado, in Madrid, where the works of the Spanish masters Diego Velázquez, Bartolomé Murillo and Francisco Goya made a lasting impression. From Madrid she travelled to Seville for the winter. There she found cheap studio space and more colourful subjects for genre paintings. Ever open to new influences in these formative years, Cassatt announced that 'one learns *how to paint* here' and adopted the 'fine and . . . simple' manner she admired in Velázquez and other Spanish realists. She abandoned the twisting, animated poses and chiaroscuro of her Italian work and darkened her palette, concentrating on capturing the reality of the figures with free touches of paint and strong tonal contrasts. These pictures of bullfighters and traditionally dressed Spanish women may appear uncomfortably posed now (see pp. 45, 47) but similar Spanish subjects had proved very popular for other painters, including Eakins and Manet, and in Spain Cassatt was able to produce exhibition pieces to be sent to both Paris and the United States for several years after her brief visit, which ended with her return to Paris in April 1873.

In Paris, Sartain and Cassatt were overjoyed to see each other again and to resume their debates on art, but their differences of artistic opinion, held with equal conviction and defended with equally uncompromising vehemence, created increasingly painful tensions within their friendship. Considering figure painting to be the highest form of art, Cassatt had shown little understanding of Sartain's achievements as a printmaker, an attitude which Sartain had resented. In their time apart, their interests had diverged still more. During her stay in Parma and Seville, Cassatt had moved further and further from accepted academic standards of preparation and finish, reflecting the teachings of Couture by generally working straight on to the canvas without making careful compositional drawings. Sartain criticized Cassatt for 'slovenly' drawing, and her criticisms were echoed by M. Luminais, who commented that Cassatt's manner was 'common', the product of too many different influences, and merely a 'talent of the brush'. Cassatt's opinion of Luminais was equally uncomplimentary. She and Sartain criticized each other to their friends, and their friendship was to collapse in bitterness in 1875. Sartain eventually returned to the United States as a recognized painter (she was awarded a gold medal at the Philadelphia Centennial Exposition in 1876) and for 33 years from 1886 she was Principal of the Philadelphia School of Design for Women.

Cassatt still had many other friends in Paris with whom she had resumed contact during this brief return. To her wide circle of acquaintances among American expatriates and students of Gérôme and Chaplin, she now added several young artists who, like her, were questioning traditional attitudes to painting. She may have been introduced to Claude Monet and Pierre-Auguste Renoir, and a small portrait of Alfred Sisley's wife from 1874 bears a personal inscription to the sitter, indicating that Cassatt's links with these independent artists were already firm enough to draw her back to Paris permanently a year later.

Mrs Cassatt travelled to Europe in the summer of 1873, and accompanied her daughter on a tour of The Netherlands, where Mary wished to continue her instruction from the old masters. She had admired works by Rubens in the Prado, and in Haarlem and Antwerp she spent several weeks copying paintings by both Rubens and Frans Hals. The honesty of expression and the bravura handling in these artists' portraits captured her attention, and a small portrait of her mother painted in Antwerp that summer demonstrates their influence: it combines a sketchy treatment of textures within a limited range of colours with a loving rendition of Mrs Cassatt's straightforward, intelligent gaze. In her path from Couture to Velázquez and Hals, Cassatt revealed her sympathy for the same models that had formed Manet's style two decades earlier. While in Antwerp she met the copyist Leon Tourny and his wife, close friends of Edgar Degas; it was very likely they who effected

Five o'Clock Tea, *c. 1880, Museum of Fine Arts, Boston.*

her eventual meeting with Degas in 1877.

When her mother returned to Pennsylvania in autumn 1873, Cassatt made a second visit to Rome. Back in the more colourful south, she again produced genre paintings – such as *A Musical Party* (see p. 49), which was admired for its luminous highlights, although it displayed a suspiciously individual approach to their application. Another result of this trip was a portrait, *Ida*, now lost, which was exhibited in the 1874 Salon. On seeing this, in the company of Tourny, Degas reportedly announced that he recognized 'someone who feels as I do'. Cassatt's enthusiasm for Degas' work also began in 1874, when she recalled seeing for the first time Degas' pastels in the window of a picture dealer on the Boulevard Haussmann. 'I used to go and flatten my nose against that window and absorb all I could of his art. It changed my life. I saw art then as I wanted to see it.'

Back in Paris in the spring of 1874, though, Cassatt had at last to consider what part she wished to play in the richly diverse Parisian art world. Many of her contemporaries were about to secure a highly visible – not to say notorious – position as opponents of the Academy with the opening of the first 'Independent' exhibition that year, at which they were slightingly dubbed the 'Impressionists'. Cassatt's own concentration on rich colour effects, naturalism and spontaneity, and her impatience with pedantic drawing, might have been expected to align her with these rebels on technical grounds. More importantly, despite having had work exhibited at the Salon, she shared with them a resentment against the official exhibition system which perpetuated the prejudices of the jurors to the exclusion of experiment in any form. She wrote forcefully on this 'enslavement', refusing invitations to act as a juror for American exhibitions in later life: 'I think the jury system may lead . . . to a high average, but in art what we want is the certainty that the one spark of original genius shall not be extinguished, that is better than average excellence, that is what will survive what it is essential to foster' (September 1905). However, despite the wealth of different artistic experiences gleaned from her travels and the decisiveness of her aesthetic opinions, Cassatt still lacked the confidence to pursue a fully independent line in her work.

Recognition by the Paris Salon meant a good deal to an American artist, and Cassatt had already been shaken by its rejection of several pictures over the years, almost certainly on the grounds of her free brushwork and light colouring. The Salon also acted as a seal of approval for the conservative art-buying public, and a young artist could hardly afford to alienate this source of income. Despite her family's prosperity, Cassatt was still obliged to support her Paris studio through sales, so for the three years between 1874 and 1877 her paintings reflected the demands of her fashionable clientele. Though never a society painter like fellow expatriates John Singer Sargent and James Abbott NcNeill Whistler (both of whom painted members of Cassatt's family), she began to produce polite drawing-room scenes like *Young Woman on a Settee with a Black Dog* and *Mrs Duffee Seated on a Striped Sofa, Reading* (see p. 51). Cassatt's interests in rendering textures and clothes make these pictures lively enough, and they sold well – especially to American buyers – but they represent one of the less convincing periods in her depictions of female life, acutely observed and attractive, but not emotionally engaging.

While she did not experience the celebrity which had surrounded her in Parma, Cassatt nevertheless became the centre of an admiring circle of artistic and other acquaintances once established in Paris. Her reputation as a brilliant conversationalist – easily communicating her own enthusiasms and breadth of interest (she was widely read in French literature and politics) – was recorded by several of those who knew her.

It was at this time, in 1874, that she met Louisine Waldron Elder, a young American resident in a *pension* run by a friend of Cassatt, Madame del Sarte. Elder – later the wife of 'Sugar King' Henry O. Havemeyer – was to become Cassatt's lifelong confidante and supporter, and their meeting inaugurated the second major strand in Cassatt's career, as an adviser to the wealthy Americans who created the United States' first great art collections. This activity began in 1875, when Cassatt persuaded the young heiress to buy a Degas pastel, *The Ballet Rehearsal*, for $100. Believed to be the first Impressionist work to have entered the United States, this acquisition was followed by the purchase of Monet's *The Drawbridge, Amsterdam* in the same year, and formed the basis of one of the finest private collections of Impressionist pictures ever made. Ever grateful to the 'fairy godmother' of her collection, Louisine Havemeyer recorded for posterity many of Cassatt's statements on art, and their correspondence gives valuable insights into the painter's complex personality and formative experiences.

Cassatt was also an influential figure to many American women artists, who were coming to Europe in ever increasing numbers. After further study at Villiers-le-Bel and a brief holiday with her family in Pennsylvania in the summer of 1875, Cassatt established a studio at 19 rue de Laval, Paris, where she received many visitors, including students. Among these was May Alcott, sister of Louisa M. Alcott, the author of *Little Women*, who arrived in Paris in 1876. Her letters home cast Cassatt in a heroic light: 'Miss Cassatt was charming in two shades of brown satin and rep, being very lively and a woman of real genius, she will be a first-class light as soon as her pictures get a little circulated and known, for they are handled in a masterly way, with a touch of strength one seldom finds coming from a woman's fingers.'

Cassatt was already perceived as part of the avant-garde movement in reaction against the values of the Academy, although as yet her links with the Impressionists were informal. Generous in providing her visitors with contacts and advice, she herself had still to make explicit the course in which she was to channel her creative energies. However, two events of 1877 were decisive in directing her future career.

The first of these was her eventual meeting with Degas, who paid a visit to her studio early that year. Possibly acting on information on her modernist sympathies from their mutual friend Tourny, he had come to invite her to exhibit exclusively with the Impressionists (or Independents, as both Degas and Cassatt preferred to think of themselves). The group's rules prohibited its members from submitting work to the Salon, which had rejected Cassatt's entries that year because, in May Alcott's view, they were in 'too original a style for these fogies to appreciate'. (She had already had the revealing experience of having a painting rejected in 1875 but accepted the next year after she had darkened the background colour.) This further failure of the Salon to accommodate her individual style was the spur she needed to commit herself to the Independents' cause. As she later told Segard, on receiving Degas' invitation 'I accepted with joy. I hated conventional art. I began to live.'

The decision was liberating, and she set to work preparing for the expected fourth group exhibition in 1878. Degas had recruited her as an artist whose style, like his own, was too individualistic to satisfy academicians, not as one who shared the distinctive radical vision of the true 'Impressionists', Monet, Renoir, Sisley, Camille Pissarro and Berthe Morisot. None of Cassatt's experiments up to that time had approached the technical innovations to be seen in the paintings of these artists on show at their third exhibition during April 1877. Her modest attempts at landscape – a favourite Impressionist subject but never significant within Cassatt's *œuvre* – indicate her fascination with their work (see p. 53), but her more typical figure painting had always relied on conventional, if freely applied, colours and modelling. Nevertheless Cassatt, whose art was always distinguished by its intellectual qualities, was eagar to absorb the sophisticated principles of her new associates.

Foreshadowing a pattern which was to structure her career, Cassatt's adoption of new techniques and media was given additional impetus by the discovery of a rich new source of imagery when, late in 1877, Mr and Mrs Robert Simpson Cassatt and their eldest daughter, Lydia, arrived to set up home permanently in France. All three had made numerous visits to Europe to see Mary in previous years, but as her parents grew older it seemed sensible that they should combine their love of French culture with a reconstituted family life in Paris. They may also have hoped to find more effective medical treatment for Lydia, who was suffering from Bright's disease – an inflammation of the kidneys. The arrival of her family meant new responsibilities for Cassatt, who had to run the household which they established at 13 avenue Trudaine, in the artists' quarter. At the same time, this new focus on domestic matters and a ready supply of willing and familiar models turned Cassatt's attention to themes with which she could readily identify.

Transplanted from Pennsylvania, the daily rituals of polite middle-class society easily took root in the avenue Trudaine: the 'At Homes' and afternoon teas, reading and horse-riding, were activities in which Cassatt's upbringing was rooted (see pp. 12, 57, 59, 66). They were also in keeping with modernist ideals on subject-matter, and the painting of modern life freed her from the need to invest her work with false drama or exotic costume. Instead she could concentrate on the formal qualities of composition and colouring necessary to capture a fleeting mood or the glance which encapsulates a personality.

Cassatt's family were instantly drawn into her working life, as models, commentators and hosts to her many artist visitors. Their letters to the family back in the United States provide a very complete idea of the trials and pleasures of her career cut loose from the stifling protection of the Salon, and they indicate the generous moral support on which she was able to depend for reassurance in times of self-doubt. The figures of her mother and sister began to appear frequently in her art, their features often dissolving into anonymity as Cassatt experimented with the effects of surface pattern, colour and light, in both oils and monochrome prints, as in the different versions of *Five o'Clock Tea* (see p. 12) or *Under the Lamp*. Meanwhile Cassatt's commissioned portraits expressed with new sensitivity the life of their subjects, with high-keyed colours and less contrived poses (see p. 63). Her attempts to employ the full range of Impressionist strategies – the fragmented image, the blurring of peripheral objects and the fusion of colour with line and modelling – followed directly from Degas' invitation to join the group. Her experiments were particularly bold when using the media with which she was less familiar, such as etching and pastel, and pastels were eventually to become of equal importance to oils in her treatment of certain subjects. Degas' example caused her to discover within herself a growing dedication to the disciplined, expressive power of drawing, and finally to the multiple possibilities of printmaking.

The period 1877–80, during which Cassatt was preparing for her shows with the Impressionists, saw the development of a close working relationship with Degas, although she was never his pupil. Despite both artists' capacity for caustic criticism, and the frequency of what

Edgar Degas, Miss Cassatt Seated, Holding Cards, *c. 1884, National Portrait Gallery, Washington, DC.*

Louisine Havemeyer termed their 'spicy estrangements', their relationship was cemented by mutual professional respect. While Cassatt's methods did not affect Degas' work profoundly, as Manet's work had been affected by his association with his sister-in-law Berthe Morisot, Degas appreciated both her decisive tastes and her work in promoting sales of Impressionist art. Pissarro remarked that 'Degas doesn't care, he doesn't have to sell, he will always have Miss Cassatt.' For her part, Cassatt valued Degas' rare words of praise throughout her life, but she guarded her fragile self-confidence by consulting him sparingly. She confided to a friend that Degas 'is a pessimist and 'dissolves' [dissout] one so that you feel after being with him: "Oh, why try, since nothing can be done about it?" ' The difficulty of the task she had set herself, to be accepted as a painter on equal terms with men, and in a movement which was constantly attacked as the resort of lunatics, was enough for even her considerable strength of character to bear, without risking Degas' sarcasm too. Even the portrait of her which Degas began in 1884 proved too direct a challenge to her self-confidence: 'it is painful to me and represents me as a person so repugnant that I do not want anyone to know that I posed for it.' Perhaps this image showed too clearly the assertive spirit which fuelled her career but also offended against her highly conservative Philadelphia upbringing, of which she was always proud. Nevertheless, her loyalty to Degas may be gauged by her outrage when, in 1878, the jury of the American section of the Exposition Universelle rejected *Little Girl in a Blue Armchair*, with which he had helped her (see p. 55).

It was the 1878 Exposition Universelle which caused the organizers of the fourth Impressionist show to postpone their own exhibition until the spring of 1879, thus allowing Cassatt a further year to prepare her contribution. Devoted to the cause of liberty which the 'Independents' represented, she declined to participate even in the first exhibition of an American anti-establishment group, the Society of American Artists, in New York in 1878. She explained to the Society's founder, J. Alden Weir, that she was too preoccupied to help him that year: 'You know how hard it is to inaugurate anything like independent action among French artists, and we are carrying on a despairing fight and need all our forces, as every year there are new deserters. I always have a hope that at some future time I shall see New York the artists ground, I think you will create an American school.' Readily though she identified with her Parisian colleagues, once established among them Cassatt dedicated valuable support to new developments in her own country: she did exhibit with the Society from 1879 to 1894, by which time New York had indeed developed as an important art market, in particular for Impressionist work.

As expected, affiliation to an avant-garde movement damaged sales of Cassatt's new work, and her father reported that by December 1878 she was forced to contemplate producing 'pot-boilers' in order to pay for her studio and models. Despite their ready emotional support, her family still insisted that Cassatt the artist be self-financing. Refusing to compromise her artistic standards, she finally assembled a group of eleven works for the 1879 Impressionist exhibition. These were relatively well received, amidst the howls of conservative critical outrage which these events now attracted as a matter of course. Representatives of American expatriate circles, from which Cassatt was becoming increasingly distanced, could see in the new art 'only the uneasy striving for notoriety of a restless vanity, that prefers celebrity for ill doing rather than an unnoted persistence in the paths of true Art . . . ' However, Cassatt's work was also singled out in favourable notices, in particular from French critics, who praised her manipulation of light and shade, her harmonious colours and the refinement of her compositions and subjects. 'There is nothing more graciously honest and aristocratic than her portraits of young women . . . ' wrote the reviewer for *L'Artiste*.

Cassatt's scenes of women in theatres and opera boxes, or quietly reading in domestic settings, approximated to favourite Impressionist themes of contemporary life, but reflected her individual approach. Degas and Renoir presented women at the theatre, whether entertainers or spectators, as objects for delectation by the viewer, packaged attractively in fine costumes, sensuous lines and colours. Cassatt's theatre-people – exclusively members of the audience – never invite or acknowledge the appraising male eye, but concentrate on their own concerns, their features masked by shade, fans or opera-glasses. She treats them as elements integral to a composition, but her detachment is far from clinical: a new psychological truth is felt within the carefully constructed image.

Cassatt's sympathy for the cause of women's rights had until now been worked out through her personal fight for educational and career opportunities equal to those afforded to men. While her progressive political attitudes were never overtly expressed in her art, they informed it in all its aspects. Rigid social codes confined Cassatt, her Impressionist colleagues Berthe Morisot, Eva Gonzalès and Marie Bracquemond, and all 'respectable' women to those spaces traditionally assigned as suitable for female activity – the nursery and drawing-room, the private garden and places of genteel entertainment. It was this limited range of contexts which Cassatt explored and amplified, adapting her techniques and subjects to ever-original compositional formulae throughout her career. Cassatt's sympathy for the scenes of female experience which she portrayed allowed her to make a virtue out of restriction, and to perfect the expression of universal emotion through the depiction of specific relationships.

While Cassatt had always focused on female subjects, she may have been influenced to capitalize on her own 'femininity' by Morisot, whom she met in 1878. She is also known to have bought a picture by Morisot in the same year. A founding member of the Impressionist group with a deep understanding of its principles, Morisot did not work closely with Cassatt, but her attitudes seem to echo the latter's practice: 'The truth is that our value lies in feeling, in intuition, in our vision that is subtler than that of men and we can accomplish a great

The Mandolin Player (Seventh State), *1889, Victoria and Albert Museum, London.*

deal provided that affectation, pedantry and sentimentalism do not come to spoil everything.' These dangers were always avoided in Cassatt's work, in which the most delicate subjects were treated with the same intellectual rigour which might be applied to abstract composition.

For her theatrical scenes, Cassatt had taken a new care over preparation – making rapid sketches of the main lines and tonal areas in small notebooks, in the manner of other Impressionists. A further impulse to experiment through finished drawings was prompted by her work on a new journal of Impressionist prints, with Degas (its chief promoter), Pissarro and Félix Bracquemond. In autumn 1879, Cassatt returned from a tour of the Alps to find her colleagues absorbed in the manipulation of different printmaking techniques to create immensely complex textures and 'colour'. Very different from the skilled but essentially unimaginative work of Sartain and Raimondi, these prints, especially Pissarro's, embodied Impressionism at its purest: divorced from the obvious association of the school with bright local colour and rapid execution, Impressionist printmaking sought to capture the same atmospheric effects by a method which was anything but spontaneous.

This reconciliation of paradoxical ends and means through the exercise of the intellect made printmaking particularly attractive to Cassatt, who even bought her own press to facilitate the work. The different stages of the process, because executed on separate surfaces, allowed her to analyze the choices an artist makes in determining where and how the marks shall be arranged and made, and where the image shall be cropped, in a way not possible while painting in her habitual manner. The necessity of producing a fully worked drawing for transfer to the printing plate, and the varied transitional states which had to be printed before the image was perfected, created a series of treatments of the same subject which

The Visitor (Preliminary Drawing), *c. 1879–80, The Cleveland Museum of Art.*

also related to later Impressionist practice in other media (represented most famously in Monet's series motifs). For the projected journal, *Le Jour et la nuit*, Cassatt produced a further opera scene, *At the Opera (No.3)*, in which the atmospheric tonal gradations and the simplification of form, worked on through several trial states, create a suitably dramatic image. This print was exhibited at the 1880 Impressionst show, possibly alongside trial proofs, as Cassatt was certainly to do later, finally acknowledging printmaking as an expressive vehicle for original compositions in its own right.

Due to Degas' inability to finish a project, so Mrs Cassatt wrote, *Le Jour et la nuit* was fated never to appear, although the prints created for it were issued separately. Degas' own contribution, *Mary Cassatt at the Louvre: The Etruscan Gallery*, used the full range of possible effects, and clearly influenced Cassatt's most Impressionistic print, *The Visitor* (see p. 19). The preliminary drawing for this positions the standing and seated figures in the same relation as in Degas' composition; in Cassatt's print this image is then reversed and strengthened, making expert use of *contre-jour* – silhouetting the woman's figure against the light – and veiling the room in stippled layers of shadow which are no less complex than Degas' own. Printmaking could clearly satisfy Cassatt's ambitious nature, although it was not until a decade later that her use of the medium was to become truly innovatory. Meanwhile, through this new skill she was able to add a further dimension to her studies of the domestic scene.

Cassatt's work continued to attract the attention of sympathetic observers at the 1880 Impressionist exhibition, most importantly that of J.K. Huysmans, a novelist and perceptive critic of the modern movements of the late nineteenth century. He may have found Cassatt's unemphasized naturalism particularly appealing, but it was her subject-matter that caught his imagination. Placing her between Gustave Caillebotte and Degas in his review of the 1880 show, Huysmans approved the tranquil bourgeois sensibility which made pictures like *The Cup of Tea* especially poignant. Like Luminais some years before, Huysmans considered that Cassatt's artistic personality was not yet clearly defined, but he noted a special quality, 'a flutter of feminine nerves' which ran through her painting, distinguishing it from that of Morisot. One of the disadvantages of projecting a specifically female understanding of one's subject, Cassatt had discovered, was that even progressive male critics were likely to base their criteria for judgement on the qualities traditionally associated with femininity. Cassatt had learned the difficulty of winning more objective criticism during her years of training, writing to Emily Sartain in the early 1870s that no woman sold pictures in America except where the motive was to patronize a woman. Nevertheless, she was becoming recognized, and she was about to encounter the fresh source of inspiration which was to shape her future output and ensure her lasting reputation.

In the summer of 1880, Alexander Cassatt, now married with four young children, brought his family to Europe to pay an extended visit to their grandparents and aunts. Alexander had enjoyed spectacularly swift promotion at the Pennsylvania Railroad, where he was now first Vice-President, and Mary was eager to channel her brother's funds into the collection of modern art which she herself could not afford. Astute in her judgements on art collectors as on art itself, she tried to interest Alexander in Degas' scenes of horse-racing: her brother owned several race-horses, whose fortunes were followed avidly by his parents through the American newspapers.

Cassatt was always to express disappointment at her family's failure to share her enthusiasms, but they did contribute to her own art in other, practical, ways. While Alexander and Lois Cassatt travelled through Europe on business, the children spent the summer with their relatives at a rented house at Marly-le-Roi. Cassatt had painted the eldest child, Edward, once before, during her last visit home in 1875; her manner had then been akin to the conservative style of Charles Carolus-Duran, Sargent's teacher, and she had not considered the picture a success. Now, equipped with Impressionist precepts of spontaneity, new models and Marly's attractive garden, she was inspired to add a new vividness to her vision of family life. This time the children were painted with a

Susan on a Balcony, Holding a Dog, *1882, The Corcoran Gallery of Art.*

true feeling for their personalities, not as miniaturized versions of formal adult portraits, although Cassatt's impersonal eye avoided cloying intimacy. Cassatt saw pictures like *Mrs Cassatt Reading to her Grandchildren* (p. 71) as technical exercises, to be perfected through disciplined reduction of the composition to essentials, like any other work no matter how personal the subject-matter.

Unlike the city apartment in which the *Little Girl in a Blue Armchair* sulked, the paintings and pastels from Marly are suffused with direct sunlight. Cassatt took every opportunity to pose her models, including Lydia and the household staff, outside; for the first time, a true *plein air* atmosphere is felt in her work and this even extends to paintings executed at the apartment, such as *Susan on a Balcony*, one of Cassatt's rare cityscapes (see p. 21). As a consequence, her palette brightened considerably, with rich greens to the fore, and she used strong highlights and shadows. Lydia's pale, fragile face is seen contrasted against backdrops of brilliant foliage, often rendered by brushstrokes which describe the growth of the plants. She reads, or crochets or sits quietly contemplating her surroundings, providing Cassatt with a calm focus within the exuberant release of colour. This effect is felt even in pictures presumably set indoors, such as *Elsie in a Blue Chair*, a dazzling pastel in blues and whites. Degas noted this change on Cassatt's return from Marly: 'What she did in the country looks very well in the studio light. It is much stronger and nobler than what she did last year.'

The pictures painted at Marly were her most successful contributions to the sixth Impressionist exhibition, in 1881, and Huysmans was now able to write that she expressed a fully original and 'sympathetic understanding of the quiet life, a profound feeling of intimacy'. Huysmans applauded her avoidance of sentimentality in her treatment of family life – a fault he detected among English painters using the same motifs. In particular, he praised her pictures of mothers and their babies, first attempted in 1880 with *Mother About to Wash her Sleepy Child.*

The visit of her young nephews and nieces may have inspired Cassatt to make further investigations into the problematic field of child portraiture: babies offered the same variety of movement as small children, challenging her observation and draughtsmanship, but they were also passive models without distracting individualistic traits. Cassatt's pictures of her family, with the exception of those specifically intended as portraits, such as *Reading Le Figaro*, had subordinated the delineation of character to the construction of overall pictorial and atmospheric effects. Mother and baby studies represented a refinement of this strategy: they were able to contain the most delicate emotions within a format that was endlessly flexible yet unchanging, and impersonal. Her few early attempts at the subject were well-received, but this important theme then disappeared for several years, to re-emerge at the end of the decade as her most characteristic interest.

The importance of the role which her family had assumed within Cassatt's life was underlined when its stability was threatened by a series of crises in 1882, which coincided with disruption in the wider world of the Impressionist group. Her purposeful routine of preparation for annual exhibitions was interrupted by internal disagreements within the group, and Cassatt followed Degas in boycotting the 1882 exhibition after a disagreement with other group members over who should be allowed to participate. This loss of an important showcase was especially serious that year, during which a slump on the Paris stock market had a marked effect on the number of investors in modern art. In America, Alexander's

The Stocking, *c. 1889, National Academy of Design, New York.*

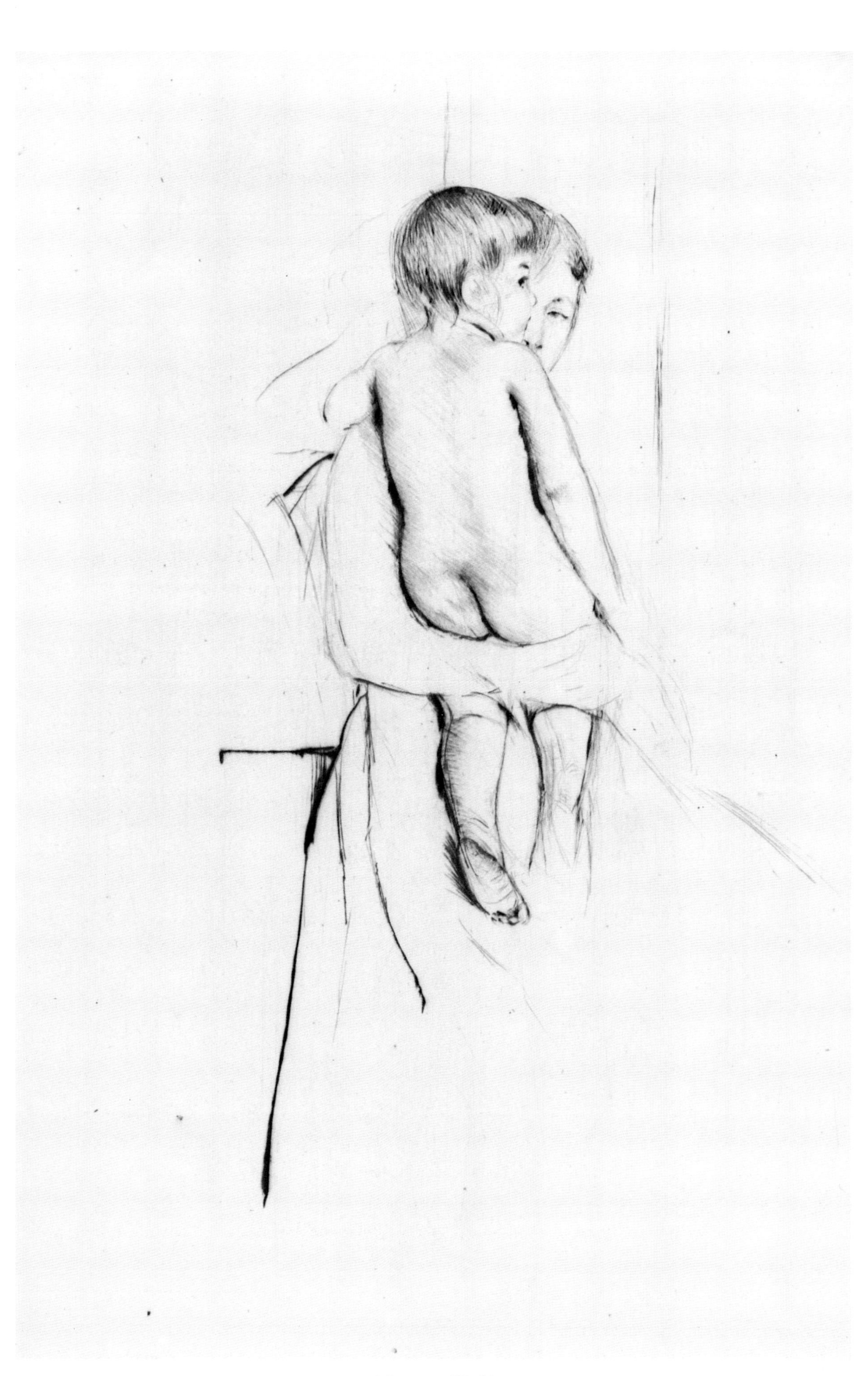

Baby's Back (Third State), *c. 1889, The Library of Congress, Washington, DC.*

career suffered a reversal on his resignation from the Pennsylvania Railroad. To add to his parents' worries, Lydia's condition became steadily worse during the course of the year. Cassatt's pictures of her engaged in quiet pursuits and in interiors, with the notable exception of *Woman and Child Driving* (see p. 59), had been tacit acknowledgements of Lydia's invalid condition. The last pictures to feature her distinctive figure, like *Lydia Working at a Tapestry Frame* of 1881, are among the most immediately touching ever produced by Cassatt. The expatriate artist was to feel the loss of family and friends keenly over the years; when Lydia died in November 1882, Cassatt was reportedly unable to work at all for six months, and could work only sporadically for a year thereafter. The Parisian branch of the family observed a two-year period of mourning, and the health of all suffered. Mrs Cassatt in particular became seriously ill, and in future a great deal more of Cassatt's time was to be occupied with caring for her ageing parents. She had to organize the household's move to 14 rue Charron and cope with her father's increasing irascibility, and trips abroad for the good of her mother's health placed heavy demands on her time and stamina.

The continuing financial slump prevented any further Impressionist exhibitions until 1886. While Cassatt maintained her links with her colleagues in the group, this loss of direction may have contributed to the startling change in her work which now occurred. This period to 1886 produced far fewer pictures than Cassatt had been used to preparing for annual exhibitions, yet during this time she was able to create some of her most distinctive portraits. She retreated indoors, and domestic articles and backdrops – picture frames, ornaments and furniture – began to appear in the paintings once more. A more severe style emerged, abandoning the rich colouring and semi-Impressionist brushwork of the Marly paintings for a new concentration on the ordering of compositional elements across the pictorial surface. Perhaps the familiar and unchanging nature of her props, which came to include above all fashionable hats and dresses, served as a comforting anchor in reality for her more daring experiments with form.

Despite their tighter reign on colour and greater reliance on tonal contrasts for effect, portraits like those of Mrs Riddle and Jennie Carter Cassatt, the artist's new sister-in-law who visited her in Europe in 1883, were no less striking than her earlier work (pp. 77, 79). Of all Cassatt's very wide circle of acquaintance, the Riddles and Jennie (a favourite with the family) were especially welcome visitors at a difficult time. Cassatt paid particular care to the delineation of their characters, which are projected strongly from within a tightly controlled composition. Free brushwork tends to be restricted to highlights relieving planes of subdued colour; the Impressionist's brilliant superficiality is replaced by an emphasis on the material.

The new laboriousness of Cassatt's procedure is demonstrated by her preparatory work for a dual portrait of Alexander and his youngest son, Robert, who made a surprise trip to Paris late in 1884, primarily to see Mrs Cassatt (see p. 83). Robbie was a fractious model, yet Cassatt was able to make two sketches of him, in pastel and oil, and several highly disciplined drypoints. It is these latter which the final picture most resembles in its dignified but slightly tense atmosphere. Oil-paintings in Cassatt's mature style were to combine a modified yet still bold use of colour with a new-found classicism developed through her discovery of drypoint (a technique in which an image is scratched directly on to a printing plate to produce prints with richer lines than those obtained by etching in acid).

By 1886, the participants in the early Impressionst

shows had developed divergent interests, and a range of styles was to be seen at the gallery of Paul Durand-Ruel, their principal dealer. Renoir had taken his treatment of bathers to monumental levels, while Degas had given the same theme a new truthfulness and awkward appeal. However, that year's sensation was caused by a group of younger artists, including Georges Seurat and Paul Signac, whom Pissarro had invited to take part in what was to be the final Impressionst exhibition. The 'Neo-Impressionists' had even more sophisticated views on the processes of vision and how to replicate them in paint, and Seurat's *Sunday on the Island of La Grande Jatte* made the work of the better-established artists appear relatively conservative. Still, financial stability was not yet enjoyed by all of the older group members, and it was Cassatt, Degas, and Morisot who underwrote the cost of the exhibition.

Even Durand-Ruel had come close to bankruptcy through his loyalty to the Impressionist cause in times of public scepticism and economic recession; in 1882 Cassatt had come to his assistance with both money and introductions to wealthy American friends, to whom she arranged sales of Impressionist work. She may also have been instrumental in gaining Durand-Ruel the invitation from the American Art Association of New York to organize a major exhibition of French art in 1886. American critics were impressed by the collection of 300 Barbizon and Impressionist works, and official recognition of the new schools followed swiftly. Cassatt was well placed to help meet the new demand for modern European art. Able to offer perceptive judgements on possible acquisitions, and valuable experience in transporting fragile goods across the Atlantic, she was to become a key figure in the export of modernist art to a newly enthusiastic market in the United States.

Cassatt had by now recovered her former energy and had developed methods and imagery which were to sustain her for the rest of her career. The unqualified admiration which her picture *Girl Arranging Her Hair* won from the supercritical Degas must have confirmed her in her choice of the manner which she now adopted (see p. 91). This picture may have been primarily an exercise in drawing and composition, but its mood also reflects Cassatt's attempts to explore more profound issues: she moves on from ladies in polite drawing-rooms to girls and mothers in the intimate surroundings of the nursery or bedroom, to the female experiences underlying their visible social roles. Possibly the loss of Lydia as a model had forced her to recast her vision of femininity, though her treatment of the female figure had always been a constantly developing aspect of her art. The unfocused, introspective look with which she had endowed many of her previous sitters also gives these new pictures a mysterious emotional quality – inviting sympathy without letting the onlooker share fully in the action. The averted gaze which had been characteristic of the opera scenes of the 1870s again allows Cassatt's female figures autonomy: they are absorbed in their own sensations as they bathe or play music or attend to a child. Cassatt began to employ a greater variety of movement and action within these pictures, developing her composite portrait of the modern woman while adding further polish to her technical skills.

By the end of the 1880s, her eclectic approach to training had endowed her with a range of techniques which could be applied to the new motifs in series. At the turn of the decade her prevailing interest was in print-making, then enjoying a revival among collectors in France and America. After her earlier experiments with aquatint, she had come to employ drypoint almost exclusively. The extreme discipline in coordinating hand and eye which the technique demanded appealed to Cassatt, who later told Segard '*that* is what teaches one to draw'.

The Parrot (Fourth State), *c. 1890, The Metropolitan Museum of Art, New York.*

'In drypoint you are down to the bare bones, you can't cheat,' she wrote later to Frank Weitenkampf at the New York Public Library. The experience refined what Weitenkampf termed her 'wise reticence in linear expression', already discernible in her drypoint studies of Robbie from 1885 and a factor in the controlled classicism of her mature paintings.

Around 1888, one of Cassatt's associates on *Le Jour et la nuit*, Félix Bracquemond, galvanized printmaking activity in Paris with three new projects: a magazine, *L'Estampe originale*, a print society, and an exhibition for the works of the new *Société des peintres-graveurs français*. Cassatt contributed three works to the first of these exhibitions, which opened in January 1889 – most significantly a pastel and a drypoint, both on the mother and child theme. Again, enthusiasm for a new technique accompanied the discovery of fresh images. For the second exhibition, in March 1890, Cassatt produced a much larger selection of work, including twelve drypoints specifically intended to be seen as a series, and some new aquatints.

Aquatint is a technique used to create areas of tone and texture within the etching process. Fine grains of resin are deposited on selected areas of the etching plate. After the grains have been fixed by heat and the plate has been etched in acid, these areas print as a grey tint. The depth of tint depends on the time for which the plate is exposed to the acid, and several aquatint layers can produce exceptionally subtle tonal effects.

Cassatt's drypoints for the 1890 show included *The Mandolin Player*, *The Parrot*, and *Baby's Back*, (see pp. 18, 24, 27). Each combines a sparing use of detail with the application of many fine lines which delicately model the figures. This gives them great charm and technical interest, but can also make them appear somewhat uneven. It was for this that Edmond Goncourt, another novelist-critic, criticized her after viewing the 1890 show: 'The admiration expressed in all the papers for Mlle Cassatt's etchings is enough to make you die of laughter! Etchings in which there is one little corner well executed, one corner out of a whole in which the drawing is stupidly heavy and the acid bite clumsy. Oh! truly this is an age that makes a religion of failures, its high priest is Degas, and Mlle Cassatt is the choirboy.' In her next series of prints, Cassatt was to employ the most characteristic effects of both drypoint and aquatint together, to create a style which was both unique and triumphantly successful.

Several other factors were to play their part in this development. The first of these was an inspirational exhibition of Japanese colour prints and other art objects, held at the École des Beaux-Arts in Paris in May 1890. Organized by the collector Siegfried Bing, the show included over 700 prints of the type known generally as *ukiyo-e*, or 'pictures of the floating world'. Exemplified by the masterpieces of Utamaro and Hokusai from the late eighteenth and early nineteenth centuries, these elegant pictures of daily life amid the courtesans and actors of urban Japan had been known in Europe for about forty years. The polychromatic woodcuts known as *nishike-e* were particularly admired, and many artists, including Cassatt, could afford to collect them. Their distinctive narrow formats, flat colouring and emphasis on a decorative surface rather than on realistic perspective were as attractive to artists as the exotic subject-matter, and Paris was in the van of a wave of '*Japonisme*' which affected European art and design for the rest of the century. Degas' treatment of Mary Cassatt's pose in *At the Louvre*, for example, may owe something to *Woman with Rearing Horse*, a page from Hokusai's huge work the *Manga*, a multi-volume book of sketches of daily life which was already known to the Impressionist group through a copy acquired by Félix Bracquemond in 1858.

Kitigawa Utamaro, Two Courtesans, One Reading a Letter and the Other Playing a Samisen, *c. 1790, Victoria and Albert Museum, London.*

The elegant lines, decorative compositions and delicate colours of Japanese prints also appealed to Cassatt, who saw in them new ways of interpreting and transforming the everyday subject-matter which she favoured. The approach of Japanese masters like Utamaro to intimate scenes of female life seemed to parallel Cassatt's own, balancing sensitive observation with the demands of pattern and technical perfection (see left). Utamaro's interest in fashion mirrored Cassatt's, and it was he who had popularized the maternity theme in Japan, with directly sensuous interpretations of the relationship between mother and child. Cassatt's recognition of an important new source of inspiration was immediate, and her enthusiasm was captured in a well-known letter to Berthe Morisot, in April 1890: '. . . we could go to see the Japanese prints at the Beaux-Arts. Seriously, *you must not* miss that. You who want to make colour prints you couldn't dream of anything more beautiful. I dream of it and don't think of anything else but colour on copper . . . P.S. You *must* see the Japanese – *come as soon as you can*.' While Cassatt's use of colour in prints had been limited, Morisot had already begun to experiment with colour lithography in 1888. Now, the linear precision and fine planes of colour seen in Japanese works allowed Cassatt to realize the full potential of the printmaking techniques she had found most sympathetic.

Morisot made another colour print after seeing the Japanese exhibits, and it seems likely that she worked closely with Cassatt in experimenting with this new medium throughout the summer of 1890. Both artists produced very similar sketches of the model used in Cassatt's colour print *The Coiffure*, a less refined, more richly atmospheric, version of which is found on p. 30. By the end of the year Cassatt was preparing a new set of prints using drypoint and colour aquatint for the third exhibition of the *peintres-graveurs*. Following her Japanese

Sketch for The Coiffure, *1890–91, National Gallery of Art, Washington, DC.*

sources, she intended the ten prints to be seen as a unit, possibly contained together in a portfolio. Within the set there can be discerned a loose sequence of everyday female activity – bathing, visiting, letter-writing – including scenes which she had not attempted before in any medium, such as *In the Omnibus* and *The Dress Fitting* (see pp. 95, 101). Presenting the prints together excluded the possibility of duplicating any theme too closely and forced Cassatt to look beyond the domestic interior to the dressmaker's and the city street.

Essential to the creation of the mood of self-containment and elegance which permeates the 'Set of Ten' was Cassatt's mastery of the procedures used. Her drypoint practice over the previous decade gave her an eye for pleasing linear effects, while the limited palettes of her most recent paintings were reflected in the simple colour schemes which gave the prints their decorative force. Cassatt's own recollection of her technique was typically understated: in a letter to Samuel Avery, already a collector of her monochrome prints, she wrote, 'My method is very simple. I drew an outline in drypoint and transferred this to two other plates, making in all, three plates, never more, for each proof. Then I put an aquatint wherever the colour was to be printed; the colour was painted on the plate as it was to appear in the proof.' Behind this basic pattern, which helps to explain the clarity of the final images, lay weeks of effort in preparing and printing trial states of each print, varying the colour combinations, adjusting the drypoint outlines and hand printing the editions. For the application of the aquatint ground and the printing of the final states, which involved the precise registration of the images from each plate, Cassatt employed the printer M. Leroy, to whom she had probably been introduced by Bracquemond. The importance of a skilled professional printer had been noted by Pissarro and Cassatt appreciated her good fortune in being able to afford Leroy's services. The editioned states of each print in the 'Set of Ten' bear the names of both the artist and her printer – a rare acknowledgement in European art, although common in Japanese prints. Between them, Cassatt and Leroy produced works which demonstrated a unique understanding of the complementary qualities of Western and Eastern aesthetics, welcomed by the reviewer for *L'Art moderne* as 'a new art that is both charming and perfectly personal'.

The exhibition of the colour prints in April 1891 marked another stage in Cassatt's professional development in two ways. For the first time she had pioneered a technique which was totally her own; secondly, she was forced by circumstance to exhibit her work independently. In 1891 the *Société des peintres-graveurs français* decided to exclude from their annual shows artists who were not French by birth. This outbreak of petty nationalism affected both Cassatt and Pissarro, who had been born in the West Indies. However, the two artists were given space in Durand-Ruel's gallery in which to display their work, and Pissarro anticipated with relish the reception of Cassatt's prints by the *peintres-graveurs* members. 'We open Saturday, the same day as the patriots who, between the two of us, are going to be furious when they discover right next to their exhibition a show of rare and exquisite works,' he wrote to his son, Lucien. 'I have seen attempts at colour engraving which will appear in the exhibition of the patriots, but the work is ugly, heavy, lustreless and commercial.' Perhaps it was this latter aspect, reflecting the rapid development of mechanical colour-reproduction processes, which prompted the Salon to ban colour prints from official shows in the same year.

To some extent Cassatt had intended the colour prints to be a commercial, but tightly controlled, means of disseminating her art to a wider public. While the prints were still directed towards an audience of wealthy connoisseurs and incorporated the painterly inconsistencies which gave them value as originals, they were also multiples which could be sold more cheaply than oils or pastels. The 'Set of Ten' was put out for sale in an edition of twenty-five by Durand-Ruel in both Paris and New York during 1891, and several museums and collectors, including Henry O. Havemeyer, Louisine's husband, acquired full sets. Sale as a set was an ideal method for the dealer to dispose of all ten prints at once, but eventually some sets were broken up and the prints were sold individually.

Durand-Ruel would have preferred Cassatt to concentrate on producing the more lucrative pastels and paintings, in particular of mothers and children, which were now heavily in demand. Despite the praise of artists and critics, appreciation for the colour prints was not reflected in the rapid sales Cassatt would have liked and, although Durand-Ruel reassured her that the Parisian market was enthusiastic, she lamented the lack of support in the United States: 'I am very glad you have any sale for them in Paris. Of course it is more flattering from an art point of view than if they were sold in America. But I am still very much disappointed that my compatriots have so little liking for my work.' In the 1890s Cassatt's complaints were to be remedied by her own country's recognition of her as a major artist, paired with a new involvement in its cultural life.

In 1892, the Chicago socialite Mrs Bertha Potter Palmer came to Paris on behalf of the Board of Lady Managers for the Women's Building at the World's Columbian Exposition, or World's Fair, which was to take place the next year. Her brief was to commission women artists to provide exhibits and decorations for the building, itself the work of a woman architect, Sophia Hayden. Mrs Potter Palmer was a collector in her own right, and she had expert advice from another American living in Paris, Sara Tyson Hallowell, one of the promoter's of the women's exhibition. Both admired Cassatt's mature, dignified presentation of contemporary female life, and while in Paris Mrs Potter Palmer bought a pastel, *Mother's Goodnight Kiss*. The development of Cassatt's themes and methods, and her dedication to the improvement of women's opportunities in her native country, made her the ideal candidate to execute one of the two murals required for the tympanum of the Women's Bulding, despite her lack of experience on large-scale projects. She was therefore commissioned to paint a decoration entitled *Modern Woman* (see p. 33), while Mary Fairchild MacMonnies, better known in America but a pupil of the French Symbolist, Pierre Puvis de Chavannes, was to work on the theme of *Primitive Woman*. Cassatt accepted the commission with alacrity, and spent the summer making extensive additions to her rented château at Bachivillers to accommodate the huge canvas. A letter to Louisine Havemeyer captures some of this enthusiasm: 'I am going to do a decoration for the Chicago Exhibition. When the Committee offered it to me to do, at first I was horrified, but gradually I began to think it would be great fun to do something I had never done before and as the bare idea of such a thing put Degas in a rage and he did not spare every criticism he could think of, I got my spirit up and said I would not give up the idea for anything.'

While Cassatt's letters of 1892 reflect her great enjoyment of the mural project, it was not an easy period. The artists were expected to produce the murals in one summer, ship them and hang them at their own expense, and were to receive the fee of $3000 only after this was done. Disagreements over the contract at one stage caused Cassatt to resign, and her opinion of the male administrators of the event was low – 'I hardly think women could be more unbusiness like than some of the

Modern Woman. *Mural for the Women's Building, The World's Fair, Chicago, 1893, whereabouts unknown, presumed destroyed.*

men are.' Eventually, however, the financial difficulties were solved, and Cassatt could concentrate on the practical problems. Her mentor, Degas had 'handed [her] over to destruction' on learning of the enterprise, and she was unable to consult him at all on its progress: ' . . . if he happens to be in the mood he would demolish me so completely that I could never pick myself up in time to finish for the exposition.'

Degas' antagonism was shared by others in Cassatt's circle, including Pissarro: in their opinion, a picture which had not been planned during the design of a building could never be truly decorative – its independent character would be too strong to serve as mere ornament. While Cassatt would have been aware of this argument, she proceeded to devise a scheme for the mural which would allow her to paint figures in much the same way as in her easel pictures. 'I could not manage women in modern dress eight or nine feet high,' she admitted. Instead, she restricted the picture area by including a wide border at top and bottom, featuring bands of gold and other colours and medallions containing the figures of small children. The remaining space was then divided by two vertical bands into three sections. Within the more manageable formats thus created, Cassatt planned three separate scenes, which were to be united through colour. The central image, *Young Women Plucking the Fruits of Knowledge*, established the outdoor setting and allowed her once again to use colours which were 'brilliant yet soft', as in old tapestries. To the left and right were smaller scenes, *Young Girls Pursuing Fame* and *Art, Music, Dancing*. Cassatt wrote that she intended the general effect to be 'as bright, gay and amusing as possible': the comic chase in the left-hand panel is an intriguing departure from the habitual dignity of her female figures.

While the mural itself can now be studied only through contemporary photographs taken to document the exhibition, it formed the core of a wide range of related work produced at the same time, which provides an insight into some of Cassatt's preoccupations. The artist may have anticipated the fate of her mural, now presumed to have been destroyed at the end of the Exposition, and regarded pastels, prints and paintings such as *Baby Reaching for an Apple* (see p. 113) as a means of preserving its spirit if not duplicating its exact form. Certainly she resented the publication of photographs of the work, which she considered vulgar.

Always an advocate of 'the modern note', Cassatt was careful to dress her models in the fashions of the day,

Detail from Modern Woman.

reportedly buying couture garments for them to ensure a contemporary feel. To balance this concentration on superficial appearance, the figures were portrayed engaged in a variety of pursuits: the fruit-pickers exuded capable strength, the seated musician a measured thoughtfulness. Cassatt was confident that she had succeeded in her aims: not primarily to create a monumental work to be hung 40 feet up in the Women's Building, but to present woman completely independent of her usual relations to the world of men. 'Men, I have no doubt, are painted in all their vigor on the walls of other buildings; to us the sweetness of childhood, the charm of womanhood [is important]; if I have not conveyed some sense of that charm, in one word, if I have not been absolutely feminine, then I have failed.' While she received the support of the Lady Managers, Cassatt was taken to task by many critics when the mural was finally installed, in particular on the grounds of the predominant dark blues and greens and the invisibility of the distant figures.

Whatever its shortcomings as public art, the *Modern Woman* mural provided a showcase for the fully developed Cassatt style. Its central image embodied many of the influences which had shaped her career. The subject-matter was in accord with the ideals of the Impressionists and the masters of *ukiyo-e* in its depiction of everyday activity and appearance, yet could also be read as a modern allegory of the woman's central role in educating future generations. It satisfied Cassatt's ambitions to paint 'pictures' while presenting relationships on an intimate scale. The attitude to femininity present within the picture was simultaneously traditional and progressive: the orchard background was in keeping with the eighteenth-century philosopher Jean-Jacques Rousseau's association of woman with passive nature, yet it presented her as actively engaged in the cultivation of civilized values. The colours recalled the richness of Renaissance paintings, while the complex patterning of the figures across the surface gained conviction from her drypoint compositions.

At the age of forty-nine, Mary Cassatt was at last ready for her first major exhibition, which was held at Durand-Ruel's gallery in November 1893. This presented 67 prints, including unfinished states and some new work in colour, 17 oils and 14 pastels. The universal appeal of her themes and the coherence of their treatment gave her work a new popularity from this time on, and preparations were immediately begun for a second – retrospective – exhibition, which was held in Paris and New York in 1895. The French government requested a picture for the nation's modern art collection at the Palais du Luxembourg, and at last her faith in European taste seemed to have been justified; in 1894 she wrote, 'After all give me France – women do not have to fight for recognition here, if they do serious work.'

Financial security was now assured for Cassatt and her mother (Mr Cassatt had died in the winter of 1891), and the artist was able to purchase her own country home with the proceeds from her increasing sales. The Château de

Beaufresne at Mesnil-Théribus, bought in 1894, was within easy travelling distance of her Paris apartment in the rue Marignan to which the family had moved in 1887, and provided new motifs as well as comfortable lodgings for her many visitors. Around this time she also began to travel to the south of France for the summer: vivid Mediterranean colours and extreme contrasts of light and shade appear in some of her paintings from 1893 and 1894, such as *The Boating Party* (see p. 117).

The success of her art after such a long period of maturation did not temper her appetite for experiment, or soften her opinions regarding the official art institutions. Nevertheless, she began to express a personal conservatism in her attitudes to younger painters, like Signac, and later Matisse, who now formed the avant-garde, and whose colour experiments seemed a betrayal of the ideals of her youth. In the 1870s she had insisted on the necessity of a European art training for American artists, but she was now equally determined to create, through private and public art collections, educational resources in the United States which would obviate the need for students to travel to the degenerate Old World.

The death of her mother in 1895 freed Cassatt of all obligations except to paint. Ironically, however, an increasing amount of her time was now devoted to guiding her many wealthy American friends around the art markets of Europe, rather than developing her own reputation. The Potter Palmers, Havemeyers, J. Stillmans and J. Howard Whittemores were all encouraged to collect 'old moderns' in addition to Impressionist work. In 1889 Cassatt opposed the successful attempts of her Impressionist friends to keep Manet's *Olympia* in France, and in 1909 she wrote to the American purchaser of another Manet, *The Execution of the Emperor Maximilian*, 'It has been one of the chief interests of my life to help fine things across the Atlantic.' In the case of the Havemeyers at least, her forthright opinions and expert eye, combined with her friends' natural acumen and enormous wealth, shaped a collection of extremely high quality. Her portrait of Louisine Havemeyer, painted while the couple were in Europe in 1886, expresses special sympathy for this intelligent, strong-minded woman (see p. 121).

Cassatt herself had not crossed the Atlantic for 23 years when she finally revisited the United States in 1898. Nevertheless, as an established artist returning to her homeland, she cannot have been gratified to read the notice of her arrival printed by the *Philadelphia Ledger*: 'Mary Cassatt, sister of Mr Cassatt, president of the Pennsylvania Railroad, returned from Europe yesterday. She has been studying painting in France and owns the smallest Pekingese dog in the world.' Cassatt's dogs were griffons.

During her 18 month visit, Cassatt worked exclusively at portraiture, in particular depicting the children of her brothers and friends with a greater attention to physiognomical detail than ever before. After her 1895 exhibition she had concentrated on the maternity theme in pastel, with the exception of a set of four colour prints produced in 1896. By this time she had switched her focus from the mother to the child and had returned to more traditional compositional formats, creating a lighter mood. While delicate hatching lines modelled limbs and faces in the prints, the pastels combined smooth areas of flesh with complex layers of luminous colour, as in *Mother Combing Her Child's Hair* (see p. 125). Her work in the United States was so admired that she gained a reputation as a society portrait artist equal in stature to Sargent, who himself recommended her for at least one commission.

Her interest in portraiture continued for a time on her return to Paris, where she depicted Madame Aude, daughter of Paul Durand-Ruel, with her children. After

Portrait of Herbert Jacoby, *c. 1905, Collection Everett D. Rheese, Columbus, Ohio.*

1900, however, her approach returned to the more generalized study of the relationship between mother and child, and to the use of oil and drypoint in addition to pastel.

Cassatt did not have a monopoly on these themes at the turn of the century: her interests reflected a vogue for studies of maternity in European and American art, promoted by such artists as Eugène Carrière. She responded to an ever-increasing demand for her child studies, and even compromised some of her high standards of finish to maintain the supply of work for sale. She also experimented briefly with art nouveau decorative techniques, applying floral and child motifs to ceramic vases (see right). Approaching sixty Cassatt was as knowledgeable as ever about the art market, and kept up with new ideas and movements in psychology, spiritualism and, increasingly, politics. She was, however, less prepared to acknowledge innovations in art itself, and she expressed particular scorn for Henri Matisse, Auguste Rodin and even Paul Cézanne, whom she had once met and admired but whose reputation now eclipsed that of her friends. She sold a Cézanne painting in her own collection to buy a Courbet, and she looked back on her association with the Impressionists with increasing pride, if decreasing accuracy: 'I . . . who belong to the founders of the Independent Exhibition must stick to my principles, our principles, which were, no jury, no medals, no awards. Our first [in fact, Cassatt's first but the Impressionists' fourth] exhibition was held in 1879 and was a protest against official exhibitions and not a grouping of artists with the same art tendencies . . . Liberty is the first good in this world and to escape the tyranny of a jury is worth fighting for . . . ' In these terms she wrote to refuse the Lippincott Prize awarded to her by the Pennsylvania Academy of the Fine Arts in 1904 – her eloquence undermined by her refusal to allow liberty of expression to the new French schools.

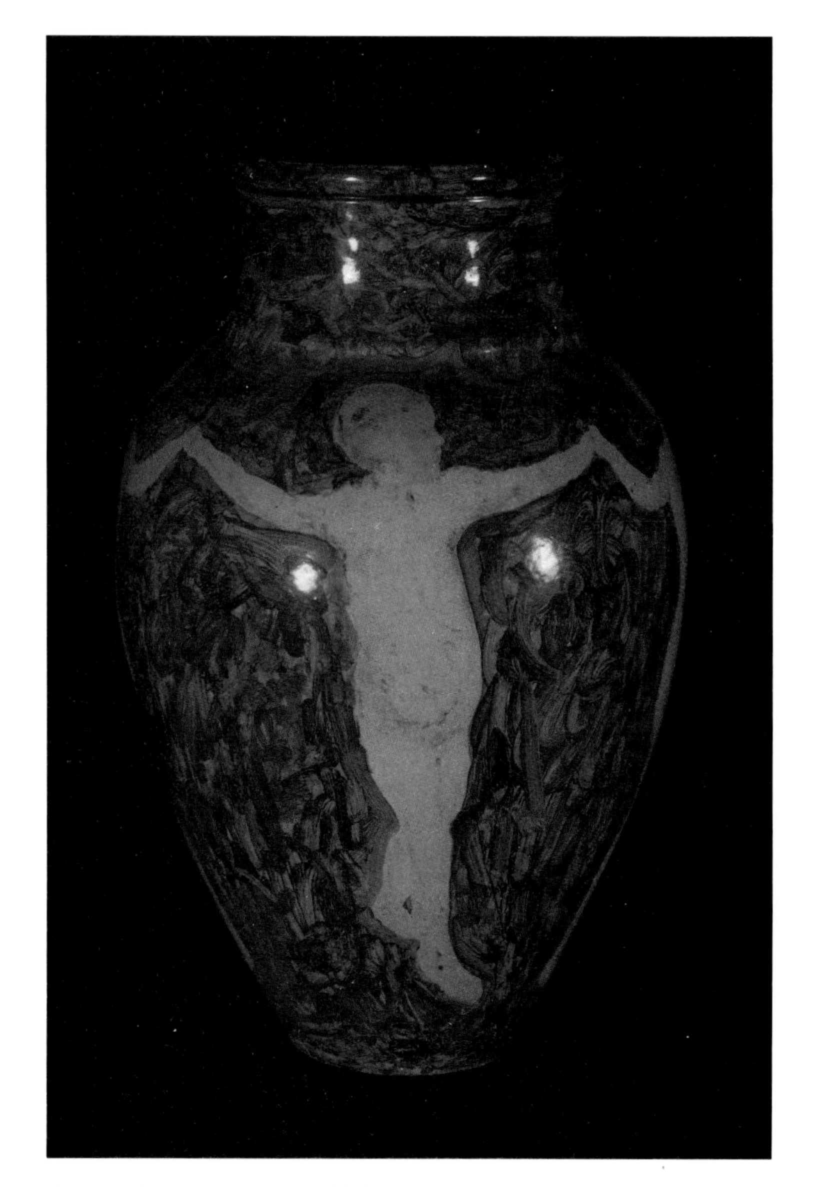

Ceramic Vase, 1903, Musée du Petit Palais, Paris.

An extended tour of Spain and Italy with the Havemeyers in 1901 provided an opportunity to reacquaint herself with the old masters who had inspired her earliest works. The influence of Velázquez reasserted itself, and in her new oil-paintings Cassatt returned to the heavy application of warm-toned paint in long, sensuous brushstrokes. The painting of flesh had never ranked high among Cassatt's interests – for her, Renoir was 'an animal' for devoting himself to it – and her nude subjects had almost always been children. Even in the two colour prints which present the female nude, *Woman Bathing* and *The Coiffure*, the pure lines are beautiful but chaste: Cassatt could never reflect the erotic aspects of Japanese prints in her own work. In pictures such as *The Caress* of 1903, however, the new approach to painting made explicit the physical nature of the maternal relationship. Cassatt had always preferred to paint mothers who cared for their children themselves, rather than entrusting them to a nurse, because they held them with a naturalness and ease which was foreign to middle-class women, despite the romanticism which now attached to motherhood. The success of such pictures in the United States prompted her to use the theme for another public art project there, this time for the Harrisburg Statehouse in Pennsylvania, in 1905, although the work she produced was never entered for the open competition (see p. 135).

By the time that Cassatt achieved real recognition as America's most distinguished woman artist, she was no longer able to contemplate leaving France. Her final ocean crossing to Pennsylvania in 1908 was traumatic, and her immediate family was dwindling fast. Alexander died in 1906 and her relationship with his widow, Lois, never cordial, distanced her from her older nieces and nephews. Her acceptance of the title of Chevalier of the Légion d'honneur, bestowed by the French government in December 1904, confirmed her position within the Parisian art scene, and her established household at the Château de Beaufresne provided a comfortable retirement from a career of ceaseless application. Though she would never return to America, her efforts on behalf of its museums and art training remained influential. Apart from her work with collectors, she received visits from many American art students and, while she never took pupils, she was as generous as ever with advice. Now she told them to abandon Europe and return home to the scenery they understood best: only work in a fixed environment could develop into satisfying art.

In 1911 the artist's brother Gardner died suddenly after a family holiday in Egypt, and deep depression curtailed Cassatt's last period of creative activity. In 1912 Achille Segard conducted extensive interviews with her for his biography *Mary Cassatt, Un Peintre des enfants et des mères*, during which she recalled with candour her career and opinions.

The outbreak of the First World War and her worsening eyesight set the seal on the isolation which was to mark the last decade of her life. The threat of invasion forced her out of Beaufresne and separated her from her faithful housekeeper, Mathilde Vallet, who was repatriated to German Alsace. Moving to her rented villa at Grasse in the south of France, Cassatt corresponded constantly, writing about the war and its privations, and about Renoir, who lived nearby: 'His wife I dislike and now that she has got rid of his nurse and model, she is always there, He is doing th most awful pictures or rather studies of enormously fat women with very small heads.' She was also able to help organize the Suffrage Loan Exhibition of Old Masters and Works by Edgar Degas and Mary Cassatt, held in New York in 1915 to raise funds for the cause of female emancipation, which she supported with Louisine Havemeyer. Degas died in 1917, and Cassatt wrote that she saw no one to replace him. She helped his niece attend to the disposal of his estate, and destroyed their correspondence.

After the war, her sight nearly gone, Cassatt returned to Beaufresne and reassembled her household, but it was now possible for her young visitors to see her as a tragic figure. Left alone by the deaths of her family and friends,

Photograph of Mary Cassatt, after 1900.

Self-portrait, *c. 1880*,
National Portrait Gallery, Washington, DC.

isolated from her country and denied a creative outlet by blindness, Cassatt was compelled to assert her independence and identity with increasingly bitter and vehement attacks on the world which had left her behind. She continued to resist accommodation with artistic developments, including those of her surviving friends: even Monet's *Waterlilies* looked 'like glorified wallpaper'.

One final incident cut her last links to the past. In 1923, Mathilde discovered a set of metal plates engraved in drypoint which, Cassatt was assured by her advisers, had never been printed. She therefore had an edition of six printed from each plate and sent two sets to Louisine Havemayer. Her friend was immediately suspicious, and her doubts about the 'new' work were confirmed by the curator of prints at the Metropolitan Museum of Art in New York, William Ivins. The images had indeed been printed over twenty years before, and reissuing them now would only damage Cassatt's reputation. The artist refused to accept that her friend and Ivins were trying to protect her, and that she could have forgotten the prints. She broke off all relations with Louisine, who nevertheless remained loyal to Cassatt for the rest of her life, and wrote a generous memoir of her when a retrospective exhibition was held at the Pennsylvania Museum in 1927.

Cassatt lived on alone, making daily excursions in her chauffeur-driven limousine; she died on 14th June 1926, aged eighty-two, and was buried near Beaufresne.

In Henry James's novel *The Portrait of a Lady* (1881) an American expatriate, Ralph Touchett, is confronted with the question 'Do you consider it right to give up your country?', to which Ralph replies, 'Ah, one doesn't give up one's country any more than one gives up one's grandmother. They're both antecedent to choice – elements of one's composition that are not to be eliminated.'

Throughout her long career, Mary Cassatt's choices were given impetus by her building on, rather than reacting against, the circumstances of her birth. Her family's wealth and culture endowed her with an education sufficient to reveal its own limitations, but her escape to Europe was not a rejection of the United States – it was a necessary preparation for the life of connoisseurship she was to dedicate to her country. She valued independence and flexibility above all else, but welcomed her family to Paris, where they sustained her innovatory art with the comforting repetition of mundane ritual. Cassatt's complex personality combined a liberal intelligence with immovable prejudices, passion with propriety, but beyond these contradictions lay the constant trait around which she built a lifetime's contribution to the history of Western art, best encapsulated in her own words: 'I am American. Simply and frankly American.'

THE PLATES

Offering the Panal to the Toreador, 1872/73

101.2 × 85.1cm, Sterling and Francine Clark Art Institute, Williamstown, Massachusetts

This picture was painted while Cassatt was in Seville, from 1872 to 1873. Attractive as a source of colourful subject-matter, so popular with established artists like John 'Spanish' Phillip and Édouard Manet, Spain also allowed art students to live relatively cheaply while benefiting from its cultural riches. *Offering the Panal to the Toreador* was accepted by the Paris Salon of 1873, thus building on Cassatt's official success with *A Mandolin Player* in the previous year. It was also exhibited at the National Academy of Design in New York in 1874.

The girl is offering the bullfighter a refreshing sweet drink, the *panal*. Cassatt poses her models with ambition, and the foreshortened right arm of the girl is especially effectively painted. However, although the sitters seem animated enough, they are not involved in any very convincing psychological situation, and it may have been dissatisfaction with the essential falseness of such studio-posed genre scenes that led Cassatt to focus on those less exotic subjects in the domestic sphere to which she had ready access and which she could understand and control.

Meanwhile, Cassatt evidently had no difficulties in approaching a theme centred on a male figure. This piece has a companion, *Toreador*, in which the man appears alone, lighting a cigarette. This second picture marked a development in the application of richly textured paint and simplified patches of colour. Both pictures had a favourable reception, but she was only rarely to include men in her later work.

On the Balcony, 1873

101 × 82.5cm, Philadelphia Museum of Art

Cassatt's capacity to assimilate the varied influences she admired is evident here. Her visit to Spain was a time of particular excitements as she discovered the 'fine and simple' style of Velázquez and other Spanish masters which had inspired Cassatt's American contemporary Thomas Eakins to produce Spanish-style genre paintings.

Cassatt had already painted a successful balcony scene in Parma the year before, *Two Women Throwing Flowers During Carnival.* In this later picture, the smooth, lyrical movements of the women seen in close-up are replaced by more realistic, awkward poses. The additional shadowy male figure is used as a compositional device to close off the background of the scene, in a way employed much later in *The Boating Party*, although here he is unusual in visibly participating in the psychological action. A similar use of the male figure could have been noted by Cassatt in Manet's picture *The Balcony*, which had appeared in the Paris Salon of 1869, and in Goya's *Majas on a Balcony*, now in New York but in a European collection at this date. Both these inspirational works depicted the modern scene of their times, but Cassatt's work is closer in spirit to the Goya, in the vivacity of its cast of characters and their involvement in a festival atmosphere. The colours are darker and more thickly applied than in her earlier Italian work, and it seems likely that she painted with only the minimum of preliminary drawing.

Her interest in the fall of light, especially her predilection for leaving faces in shadow, was to recur soon after in her Parisian opera pictures. This, together with the technical difficulties presented by the positions of the heads, indicates that Cassatt was setting herself deliberate challenges (here of foreshortening), as she would later do with her ceaseless drawing practice. This rigorous self-training was hard on both the artist and her sitters, as she acknowledged with good humour. She wrote to Emily Sartain, then in Paris, that her model had 'asked me if the people who pose for me live long'.

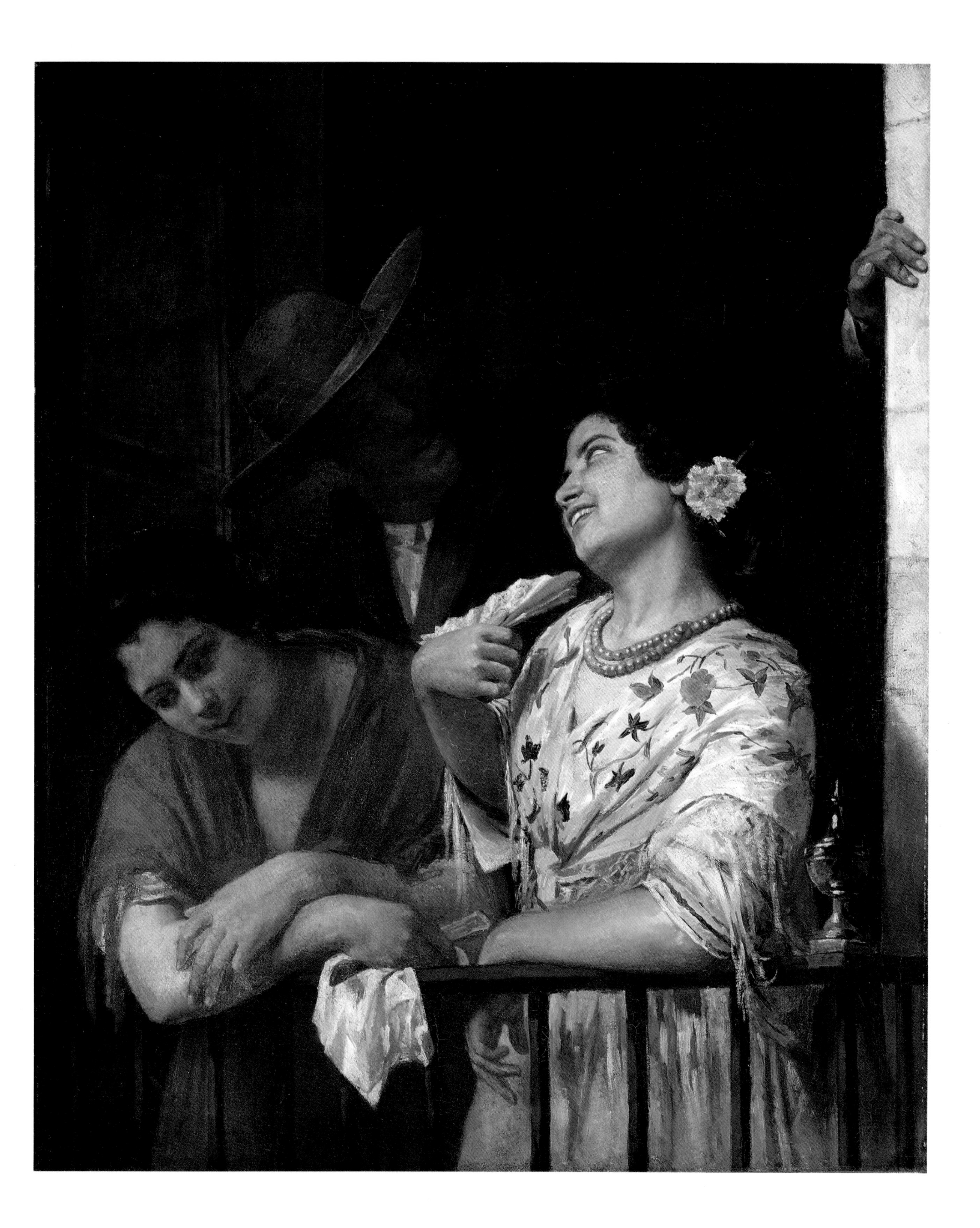

A Musical Party, 1874

96.4 × 66cm, Musée du Petit Palais, Paris

From the very earliest stages of her independent professional career, Cassatt was eager to find recognition for her work in her own country, shipping pictures there for exhibition and using a network of acquaintances to secure dealers and buyers. Her unsatisfactory Philadelphia dealer, Teubner, wanted to keep this particular work as payment in kind for his services. It was exhibited in Paris, at the 47th Annual Exhibition of the Pennsylvania Academy in 1874, and in Boston in 1878.

A Musical Party was painted during Cassatt's return visit to Rome, after her mother had left Europe for the United States in autumn 1873, and represents the fluid nature of her artistic personality at the time. The extreme tonal contrasts from background to foreground in this genre piece have been compared to the style of Gustave Courbet, the rebel Realist whose work she admired all her life. The influence of the Spanish old masters is also evident in the handling of the paint, in particular on the highlights of the ruched pink dress.

Emily Sartain, whose relations with Cassatt were already showing the strain of their arguments over artistic differences, commented on the picture as: '. . . superb and delicate in colour . . . The light on the chest of the foreground figure, a blonde, is perfectly dazzling. It is as slovenly in manner and in drawing as her Spanish pochades, however.' A *pochade* was a sketch, and Sartain, whose original talent was for engraving, had little sympathy for the impressionistic tendencies which her friend was demonstrating. The admiration in her assessment is also tangible, however. Cassatt's colour sense and her skilful manipulation of light effects were already well developed, and her approach to certain themes was beginning to emerge in its characteristic form, with the attention focused on the harmonious relationship of two young women engaged in a suitably feminine pursuit. The man has been relegated to a shadowy background presence, a spectator who redirects our eye to the foreground action. The picture uses its slightly elongated format to good effect: the patterning of gradually lightening tones from top to bottom on the surface creates some depth within the scene, although the most forceful impression is of the physical closeness of the little group.

Mrs Duffee Seated on a Striped Sofa, Reading, 1876

35 × 27cm, Museum of Fine Arts, Boston

Despite the loyalties to the United States which she was later to demonstrate, once settled in Paris Cassatt tended to keep her distance from the city's American expatriate community. However, the mid-1870s saw her struggling to support her studio, and to do this she had to produce the 'pot-boilers', including commissioned portraits, which, her father later reported, she could not 'bear the idea of being obliged to do'.

However, Mrs Duffee's picture relates not only to the conventional charms of other contemporary works, such as *Young Woman on a Settee with a Black Dog*, with which it shares a setting and colouring, but also to Cassatt's considered depictions of the quiet and peculiarly female pursuits of the leisured middle classes in such paintings as *Young Girl with a Portfolio of Pictures* and *The Reader*, both of which project a quality of self-containment that reflects Cassatt's own intellectual independence and strength. Her own love of reading earned her a reputation for learning and an ever-expanding circle of 'litterary people' [sic], as Mr Cassatt wrote. The motif of reading recurs among paintings of the early 1900s, in which Cassatt portrays her anonymous readers in educative or communal roles, as in *Family Group Reading* or *Two Women Reading*, both of 1901. This development may have been linked to the artist's own changing activity, which came to centre on the communication of her knowledge and opinions to art collectors and suffrage campaigners alike, after a long period of dedicated self-training.

M. S. Cassatt
Paris

Poppies in a Field, c. 1874–80

26.4 × 34.5cm, Philadelphia Museum of Art

Landscape is exceptionally rare in Cassatt's *œuvre*, and this sets her apart from the Impressionist mainstream, in the company of Degas who described himself as the 'indoor Impressionist' who, given the chance, would have had the *plein air* painters shot. Such landscapes as exist are often sketches from her tours around Europe, and figures are generally present.

Nevertheless, the loose date of this painting places it between the year of the first Impressionist exhibition and her participation in the fourth exhibition, when the principles of the group had their strongest influence over her. It was therefore natural for Cassatt to experiment with the form. The poppy-field was a motif which Monet and Renoir were treating in the same period; it lent itself to the shimmering surface effects of broken Impressionist brushwork and the application of bright local colour. Cassatt has divided the scene into a blank sky, on which the heads of the distant figures barely impose, and a bright busy field of colour, composed of short strokes of reds, greens and blues. This may represent a foretaste of the interest in juxtaposing pattern and planes of colour which can be seen in her pictures of the 1880s and, even later, in her prints.

Interestingly, in the light of the central importance of children later in her career, Cassatt allows a child to occupy the foreground, lost in its investigation of flowers and grasses.

Little Girl in a Blue Armchair, 1878

89.5 × 129.8cm, National Gallery of Art, Washington, DC

This is the only known work to have been a collaboration between Degas and Cassatt. In a letter to the art dealer Ambroise Vollard, in 1903, Cassatt recalled, 'I had done the child in the armchair, and he found that to be good and advised me on the background, he even worked on the background – I sent it to the American section of the Grand Exposition . . . but it was refused. Since M. Degas had thought it good I was furious especially because he had worked on it – at that time it seemed new, and the jury consisted of three people, of which one was a pharmacist!'

This taste of rejection, after a period of acceptance by the art establishment, contributed to Cassatt's lifelong distrust of juries. Temperamentally of the Independent group before Degas' invitation to join it, Cassatt now experienced the practical drawbacks of rebellion. Nevertheless, *Little Girl in a Blue Armchair* shows her determination to recast her subject matter in avant-garde fashion.

The brushwork is already confidently free, both in the treatment of the child's lacy dress and in the patterned upholstery, to which Degas may have contributed. Elsewhere, her debt to Degas' use of asymmetry and empty space is clear, and the background is untypical of her work in its extent and detail. The little girl's fractious boredom may be explained by the emptiness of this room, which, despite its elegant furnishings and the hint of sunlight from the apartment balcony, isolates her and her pet in their vast armchairs amid a sea of blue carpet. The child's formal clothes and squirming pose suggest a Sunday afternoon of enforced inactivity. Even the lap-dog sulks sleepily. Despite her own tendency to inflict long sittings on her young models (this girl was the daughter of friends of Degas), here Cassatt demonstrates a charming sympathy for the trials of childhood.

This was painted in the same year that Renoir began to gain public acceptance, with his *Madame Charpentier and her Children*, in which his young sitters are posed with a more conservative sweetness and formality, a conscious sentimentality which Cassatt was always to resist.

Mary Cassatt

Reading Le Figaro, c. 1878

104 × 83.7cm, Private Asset Management Group, Inc., New York

Cassatt's mother had always been one of her most valued supporters, travelling with her during her early studies in Europe and writing perceptively about Mary's projects. She was also the model for some of Cassatt's strongest portraits, of which this painting makes claim to be the finest. The picture won approval from the whole family, and was sent back to Alexander in Philadelphia with a note from Mr Cassatt: 'I hope you will be pleased with the portrait, in fact I do not allow myself to doubt that you will be . . . Here there is but one opinion as to its *excellence* . . . '

In 1879, *Reading Le Figaro* was exhibited by the Society of American Artists in New York, where it won critical acclaim: 'Among the technically best pictures in the entire collection was Miss Cassatt's portrait, a capitally-drawn figure of an agreable-looking, middle-aged lady . . . It is pleasant to see how well an ordinary person dressed in an ordinary way can be made to look . . . '

Painted just after her parents' move to Paris in 1877, the picture demonstrates Mrs Cassatt's rapid acclimatization to her new surroundings. The Parisian newspaper symbolizes her adopted country and situates her within the intellectual and political life of France in a way usually confined to depictions of men. Cassatt too was having to come to terms with her changed cultural surroundings; this picture affirms her new Impressionst allegiances in its use of the everyday and its robust, truthful representation.

Colours and forms are softer than before, although Cassatt's interest in contrasting patterns and planes still underlies the composition. Mrs Cassatt's rounded shoulders are echoed and strengthened by the back of the armchair, while her head is centred against the plain creamy wall. The great expanse of white dress gives the figure a solid, even monumental aspect, despite the unassuming, self-absorbed pose. The latter is reinforced by the mirror reflection, which adds complexity to the play of angles and spatial depth and counteracts the surface spread of pale tones. In these ways Cassatt avoids blandness or crudity, modulating between dark and light tones with great control.

Mary Cassatt

Woman and Child Driving, 1879

89.3 × 130.8cm, Philadelphia Museum of Art

This painting is unusual in showing a relatively wide expanse of outdoor background, receding into the green spaces within the woods of the Bois de Boulogne. However, the central scene itself is severely cropped, another indication of the influence of Degas, with whom Cassatt was working most closely at this time. (The sitters include one of Degas' nieces, Odile Fevre.)

Despite her open-air theme, Cassatt treats the figures with a static formality – the little girl's pose and Lydia's grip on the whip and reins are tense and rigid, and the whole composition has the self-conscious feel of a contemporary photograph. The little groom is an anonymous foil to the psychologically profound female portraits, and in this the picture's mood finds an echo in the later *The Boating Party*, in which the female figures are similarly divorced from the half-obscured man, both in terms of the group's arrangement and in their expressions of self-absorption. All this negates the sense of movement which the subject would seem to require. The asymmetry goes some way to suggest a forward movement of the figures from right to left, but the lack of interest in the right-hand side confines our attention to the figures.

On 18th December 1879 Mrs Cassatt wrote to her grandson Robbie, 'Your Aunt Mary is so fond of all sorts of animals that she cannot bear to part with one she loves. You would laugh to hear her talk to Bichette our pony . . . she . . . painted a picture of your Aunt Lydia and a little niece of Mr Degas and the groom in the cart with Bichette but you can only see the hindquarters of the pony.' Here the animal is simply a background element in a study of a woman and child, consistent with Cassatt's later predominant themes. The cart had been bought recently from a trust fund established for the older Cassatts by Alexander, and the painting reflects the comfortable family life, with its characteristic middle-class rituals like a weekend drive in the Bois de Boulogne, which they had quickly established in Paris.

Mary Cassatt

At the Theatre (Lydia Leaning on her Arms, Seated in a Loge), c. 1879

55.4 × 46.1cm, The Nelson-Atkins Museum of Art, Kansas City

This pastel represents the culmination of a series of pictures centred on the atmosphere of the theatre or opera box which Cassatt explored when her involvement with the Impressionist group was at its most enthusiastic. The theme satisfied various Impressionist interests, most particularly in the effects of light (here artificial) and in the common pursuits of the modern city. This picture was also a relatively early exploration of the expressive qualities of pastel, demonstrating Degas' influence most clearly in the varied use of the medium, smoothed down to suggest the sheen of the model's bared shoulder but applied in slashing diagonals in the background and at the left of the skirt to add energy to an already assertive pose.

Cassatt was quick to realize the possibilities afforded by placing a mirror within a composition, enabling her to show a figure from different angles and to repeat key lines and shapes. A distinctive feature of Cassatt's opera pictures is her use of a curve, created by the back of a chair or by tiers of seats, to strengthen or balance the line of the sitter's shoulders, or to create a bold decorative background. Here, both the divan and the reflection in the mirror enhance the sweeping movement within the image, from the chandelier to the clasped hands. Even in works where the immediate sensations are triggered by colour, Cassatt displayed the interest in line which would eventually lead to her abandoning extreme Impressionist effects in favour of precision and clarity. The light also falls from top left to bottom right, illuminating the sitter's beautiful red hair while leaving her face in shadow, a quiet passage within an image of great animation and excitement. By veiling what we might have expected to be the focus of the picture, Cassatt maintains a certain detachment from the model and centres the interest in its exhilarating colour effects.

The identification of Lydia as the model has been disputed. The pose struck here was the same as that in which Cassatt was represented by Degas in the portrait which she rejected (see p. 16). She may have felt it suitable for depicting an anonymous figure at the theatre, but not for a portrait of a respectable woman like herself. Only in this instance did she deny the truth of an image, a seemingly accurate reflection of her opinionated personality.

Portrait of Moïse Dreyfus, 1879

80 × 63.3cm, Musée du Petit Palais, Paris

Only during the early years spent establishing herself among the Impressionist group in Paris did Cassatt produce major male portraits. These were of her family and friends and of close associates of the Impressionist circle, such as the Irish writer George Moore and the artist Marcellin Desboutin. In general, her *œuvre* excludes male figures, or tends to reduce them to anonymous compositional elements.

However, this picture of the friend and art collector Moïse Dreyfus is a sensitive portrayal of individual personality. Although the pose is formal, the confident use of pastel and the unstuffy communication of the sitter's smile immediately point to Degas' influence over the artist, which was at its height in practical terms at this time. (According to her first biographer, Achille Segard, a portrait by Cassatt of her mentor was destroyed.) However, Cassatt has elected not to follow the example of several Impressionist portraits of successful men (including Degas' contemporaneous studies of the writers Edmond Duranty and Diego Martelli) which surrounded their subjects with their everyday possessions. Instead, Dreyfus' dark business-coat and the neutral background focus our scrutiny on his face. This has a luminous quality which might be compared to that achieved in a different medium in the portrait of Mrs Riddle (see p. 79). Short, diagonal strokes of pastel model rather than outline the features. The eyes behind their delicately drawn spectacles have a diffuse, slightly myopic but direct gaze.

In a change of emphasis brought about by exposure to portraits by Manet, Degas and others, Cassatt reduces pattern and decoration to a minimal strip of visible upholstery. Interest is held by the subject himself, and by the subtly complex shading behind him.

The portrait of Dreyfus was among Cassatt's entries to the fourth Impressionist exhibition, in 1879. It suffered severe damage during the Second World War.

At the Opera, 1879

80 × 64.8cm, Museum of Fine Arts, Boston

Probably the first of Cassatt's Impressionist subjects to be seen in the United States, this is the boldest of all her treatments of the opera motif, in its limited colour scheme of red, black and bleached gold, the use of a repoussoir figure, directing the viewer's eye into the picture, and, most of all, in the depiction of a woman as an *active* onlooker, although she may also be the subject of male scrutiny. Cassatt's other opera scenes portray less self-possessed women, sitting demurely behind their fans, not leaning forward to engage the spectacle as here, or in *At the Theatre* (see p. 61).

Cassatt consciously worked towards the effects of contrast and pattern she achieved here through a series of preliminary drawings. These show her blocking out the main areas of tonal contrast, paying particular attention to the juxtaposition of black and white in the foreground figure and the distant boxes behind her, with a transitional area of warm tones in the face. Cassatt's use of sketches apparently executed at the scene was a working practice acquired from the Impressionists. Unlike the detailed academic drawings she had been taught to make in Philadelphia, these small sketches allowed her the greatest freedom to experiment with a composition's basic structures.

A consummate example of Cassatt's Impressionist phase, *At the Opera* combines a popular theatrical subject (favoured by Degas in particular, but also by Renoir in his *First Outing*) with a totally individual approach to its content. The bold use of black, and the sitter's self-possession, recall Manet. This woman is not an object for appreciative scrutiny; her sombre day dress does not offer her up as a pleasing spectacle, while her foreground position ensures that she shapes the picture, dictating its action and scale. The pattern created by her arms and bonnet ribbon creates angular black contrasts to the gleaming sweep of the circle, looking forward to the tonal organisation of portraits from the mid-1880s. Like other Impressionists, Cassatt has noticed that focusing on one object blurs peripheral vision, and the man who inspects the principal figure through his opera-glasses is firmly distanced as a summarily indicated marginal figure, while we ourselves are placed in a subordinate position to the spectacle which occupies her independent attention.

The Cup of Tea, c. 1880

92.4 × 65.4cm, The Metropolitan Museum of Art, New York

Cassatt exhibited this painting in the Impressionist show of 1881, where she received particularly appreciative comments from the critic and novelist J. K. Huysmans:

> '. . . Here is family life, painted with distinction, and with love.
>
> 'In this group of works by Mlle Cassatt there is an affectionate understanding of quiet domesticity, a heightened sense of intimacy. In . . . *The Cup of Tea*, a smiling woman, dressed in rose coloured clothes, sits in a chair, holding in her gloved hands a cup of tea . . . these works accentuate the same note of tenderness, and exude a delicate fragrance of Parisian elegance.
>
> 'This indeed is the most characteristic quality of her talent, that Mlle Cassatt, who, I believe, is an American, paints French women, but manages somehow to introduce into her Parisian interiors an 'at home' feeling. She has succeeded in expressing, as none of our own painters have managed to do, the joyful peace, the tranquil friendliness of the domestic interior.'

The arrival of Cassatt's parents and sister in Paris in 1877 had changed her life irrevocably, but she immediately put their familiar presence to good use. Cassatt reinvented her amenable sister Lydia according to the mood and subject she was intent on capturing. Here Lydia is the delicate invalid, swaddled in fleecy ruffles, her shadowed complexion the foil for her pink and white garments and an audience of pot plants. The everyday objects of the family apartment were likewise an infinitely flexible resource which she could handle confidently, knowing their peculiar qualities and how these might best serve her artistic aims. Cassatt always made a virtue out of the limitations placed around her ambitions, repeating motifs and working in series throughout her career, and to the last advising her pupils that the artist must work 'in a fixed environment, and not change it very often.' Peaceful domestic ritual was therefore a congenial motif, and a key element in the life which sustained her art.

Self-portrait, c. 1880

33 × 24cm, National Portrait Gallery, Washington, DC

Cassatt used water-colour almost exclusively for rapid sketches of subjects to be worked up into finished oils or pastels later. This self-portrait is unusual in its detail and expressiveness, and notable for the role in which Cassatt casts herself. The face is delicately handled, despite the heavy shadows necessarily cast by the hat. Unusually, nuances of shading on the face, and the edges of cuff and collar, are indicated through lines, although the surrounding brushwork demonstrates her habitually dashing style.

Usually uneasy as a subject for portraiture herself (as opposed to posing anonymously on occasion for Degas), Cassatt here appears self-possessed, her look direct. The single faint blue line which cuts off her figure to the right is enough to show her as an artist in traditional pose before an easel or drawing-board. Through this pose she relates herself to that ancient line of artists, most famously Rembrandt but more recently including Cassatt's hero Courbet, who had depicted themselves in similar fashion, with the tools of their trade. Women painters too, including the Italian, Artemisia Gentileschi (*c.* 1593–1652) and several eighteenth-century French portraitists, had employed this strategy to assert their professional identities. In these self-images it is the audience who are scrutinized by the artist's eye, not vice versa, and this reversal of roles between observer and object within Cassatt's picture allows her figure the penetrating gaze of the artist.

Simultaneously, and perhaps confusingly, Cassatt also chooses to depict herself as a fashionable young woman, typically the focus of a male audience's scrutiny and admiration. The presence of her large yellow hat bears witness to her wide-ranging interest in fashion. She always kept her Philadelphian sisters-in-law informed on the latest Parisian modes, and was careful to dress her models in clothes which would contribute both decoration and modernity to her pictures of women. Cassatt's decision to pursue a career rather than marriage and motherhood made her contact with these conventional attributes of female existence more, not less, important to her – essential reference points in her exploration of modern truths.

m C

Mrs Cassatt Reading to her Grandchildren, 1880

55.7 × 100cm, Private collection

In the summer of 1800, Cassatt and her family played host to her brother Alexander, his wife, Lois, and their four children: Eddie, Katherine, Robbie and Elsie. A house in the country was rented for the summer, and Cassatt had the opportunity to put into practice her Impressionist principles more thoroughly than ever before.

On a technical level she seems to have been particularly interested in the manipulation of light, here on the clothes, the window-frame and the pages of the book. Cassatt depicts her mother reading to the three younger grandchildren by an open window. The scene is not, therefore, in the open air, but the location still allows her to use bright patches of sunlit colour and white to achieve effects associated with *plein air* painting.

Many of the Impressionists used their immediate families as models, so enhancing the mood of informality and spontaneity that they sought, and Cassatt's intentions were certainly more practical than commemorative in making use of her guests. The direct narrative treatment of the subject, concentrating on a common theme of childhood rather than on portraiture, makes this a genre picture, although this was not how it appeared to Cassatt's family. While it was being shown at the 1881 Impressionist exhibition, Mrs Cassatt wrote to her granddaughter Katherine: 'Do you remember the one she painted of you & Rob & Elsie listening to me reading fairy tales? . . . A gentleman wants to buy it but I don't think your Aunt Mary will sell it – she could hardly sell her mother & nieces & nephew I think –' Nevertheless, Cassatt was made of sterner stuff and duly sold the painting to Moïse Dreyfus (see p. 63); under pressure from her family, she later had to buy it back to give to Alexander.

Lydia Working at a Tapestry Frame, c. 1881

65.5 × 92cm, Flint Institute of Arts, Flint, Michigan

Although the titles of many of Cassatt's pictures identify her older sister, Lydia, as the subject, Cassatt was not always concerned to create an accurate likeness, instead regarding her model as one element in an exercise in composition or colour. However, while Lydia's dress, her left hand and arm and the background are freely rendered, her face is here portrayed with a detail in expression which totally convinces us of its accuracy. This painting is an intensely personal representation, made all the more poignant by its circumstances: it was painted in the last year of Lydia's life, before her death from Bright's disease on 7th November 1882. This loss had a crushing effect on Mary. When Lois Cassatt visited the bereaved family shortly after Lydia's death, she reported Cassatt's depression: 'She has not had the heart to touch her painting for six months and she will scarcely now be persuaded to begin . . . '

The painting demonstrates Cassatt's commitment to the Impressionist group at this time, and her confidence with its techniques. Her brushwork is very free, and the light filtering in from the left is wonderfully suggested as a milky mist, creating from a simple domestic scene a mysteriously romantic vision, its protagonist completely absorbed by her craft while the outside world is reduced to an undefined glare. Cassatt's strength of mind and artistic force also find expression through the jutting diagonal of the tapestry frame itself, carving out space for the image. The neat-featured, slightly sallow needlewoman gives focus to the whole. While following the pattern of many of Cassatt's pictures of women engaged in domestic tasks or specifically female roles, this understated celebration of female power through creativity is infused with a special tenderness.

Susan Seated Outdoors, Wearing a Purple Hat, c. 1881

69.7 × 92cm, Manoogian Collection

Susan was one of Cassatt's favourite models of the early 1880s. She also appears in *Susan Comforting the Baby* and *Susan Seated on a Balcony, Holding a Dog* (see p. 21), in which Cassatt combined the *plein air* method with one of her very rare views of the Parisian cityscape. She is believed to have been a cousin of Mathilde Vallet and a member of the household which Cassatt and her parents established in Paris. As such, she was a part of the world of familiar faces and objects which the artist believed to be essential to the forming of her individual vision, and which provided the raw material for her most expressive works.

The setting here could be the garden of the rented house outside Paris which the family took in the summer of 1880. The arrangement of the sitter against the path and the border of greenery recalls other portraits of Lydia Cassatt from this year. Preoccupied with Impressionist colour theories, Cassatt uses thick, stabbing brush-strokes to blend multiple shades of green into a richly textured backdrop for the pale young face. Particular care has been taken with the curve of the garden seat, its luscious colour pushing it into our view and emphasizing it as an abstract form detached from its representational function. A similar care over the effects of objects can be seen in the *Portrait of Herbert Jacoby* (see p. 36), in which the back of the armchair echoes the curve of the boy's mouth.

Cassatt seems to have returned to this type of detached treatment of the portrait subject in her pictures of children after 1900. These were often primarily colour exercises, which required their sometimes anxious-eyed models to be dressed in elaborate hats and all-enveloping clothes. Nevertheless, the fragile Susan holds her own here as the quiet centre of an explosion of colour in which Cassatt has employed green, usually a restful pigment, as a vehicle for visual excitement.

Portrait of a Young Woman in Black (Mrs Gardner Cassatt), 1883

80 × 64cm, The Peabody Institute of Baltimore, on indefinite loan to the Baltimore Museum of Art

This is a portrait of Jennie Carter Cassatt, the wife of the artist's brother Gardner. Jennie and her children proved to be among Cassatt's favourite models in her later work, and Cassatt kept this picture in her personal collection until old age. It may be to this that she referred in a letter of September 1885 to her elder brother, Alexander: 'I will send the portrait [of their father on horseback – see p. 87] to Gard as I have never given him a Portrait of Father & he is disgusted because I won't send him Jennie's portrait.'

Cassatt uses various strategies to overcome the deadening effect of black in this, one of the most animated of all her depictions of adults. The twist of the sitter's body and the angle of her head contribute to the sense of movement, while the highlights at her neck and the sheen of her pink lips lift the sombre costume, linking it to the chintzy decor of Cassatt's apartment. The arc of the fan on the back wall is also to be seen in the drypoint *The Mandolin Player* (see p. 18). Here it is part of a sophisticated play with various framing devices – the hat, the veil, the fan and the fan's mount – none of which can contain the energy of the smiling head. Turned to the light, Jennie's face is still radiant underneath its veil of grey.

Jennie Cassatt's black dress may mark the family's mourning for Lydia, who had died the year before, but 1883 marked another loss for the artist: that of Manet. The portrait instantly recalls the work of this master, not only in the simple elegance of its composition and the predominance of un-Impressionist black, but in the vitality of its portrayal of an individual female personality.

Lady at the Tea Table, 1883–5

73.4 × 61cm, The Metropolitan Museum of Art, New York

Unlike her compatriot and acquaintance John Singer Sargent, Cassatt did not cultivate a reputation as a portrait painter. Her unwillingness to undertake commissions from individuals may have been intensified by the upsetting circumstances surrounding this work.

The sitter was Mrs Robert Moore Riddle, a first cousin of Cassatt's mother, whose daughter, Annie Scott, was also the artist's friend. While in Europe, they had given Cassatt a tea and coffee service in blue Canton china which she had admired in their presence. Cassatt decided that a portrait was the only possible repayment, although her mother foresaw difficulties in a letter to Alexander: 'As they are not very artistic in their likes & dislikes of pictures & as a likeness is a hard thing to make to please the nearest friends I don't know what the result will be – Annie ought to like it in one respect for both Degas and Raffaëlli said it was "la distinction même" and Annie goes in for that sort of thing . . . '

Degas and J.-F. Raffaëlli's appraisal is clearly appropriate. The sitter is given calm authority over a carefully composed scene, in which Cassatt already demonstrates an appreciation of flat areas of heavily contrasted tones, learned from Japanese prints. (Degas and Raffaëlli were also among those most closely associated with Cassatt's printmaking activities.) Cassatt here returns to Manet's influence in posing spatial questions – the foreground and background are unified in tone, while the frames on the wall serve contradictory functions, focusing attention on the head they surround and retreat behind and providing a flattening surface pattern. The depiction of Mrs Riddle's elegant hand is also treated with a summary brilliance which refers back to Manet's handling of paint.

Short parellel brushstrokes over the face contribute a diffuse radiance and an air of introspection common to many of Cassatt's sitters, offsetting the monumental expanse of her dress, as emphatic a triangle as is to be found in any Renaissance papal portrait.

Distinguished or otherwise, the picture found no favour with Mrs Riddle's family, who declared the nose too big. Cassatt was disappointed, but was not about to accept the judgements of amateurs: 'I did it so carefully and you may be sure it was like her.' She wrote later that 'I never wanted to see it again,' and she kept the picture hidden in her own collection until 1914, when Louisine Havemeyer persuaded her to exhibit it. *Lady at the Tea Table* caused a sensation when shown and, after bids from the French state collections, Cassatt finally offered it to the Metropolitan Museum of Art in 1923.

Two Children at the Seashore, 1884

97.6 × 74cm, National Gallery of Art, Washington, DC

These robust, rosy-cheeked little girls form an interesting comparison to their counterparts in the child pictures from other stages of Cassatt's career, both earlier and later. They show none of the discontent of the *Little Girl in a Blue Armchair* (see p. 55), nor the apprehensiveness of *The Sisters* or Robbie Cassatt (see pp. 83, 85). Instead, they hold our attention effortlessly, indifferently, and their activity appears independent of adults, whether mothers, onlookers or the artist herself. Nevertheless, they share the rounded features and placid natures typical of the children Cassatt chose to depict in the 1890s. Again a high viewpoint and the narrow format push the figures forward to fill the centre ground. Despite the unusually open setting, Cassatt's interest is very clearly in a portrait subject. The hazily distant sea with its boats is treated sketchily; the beach is merely a smooth blank background for the strong tonal contrasts and solid colouring – dark blue and white, pale yellow and deep red – of the figures.

Mary Cassatt

Alexander J. Cassatt and His Son, Robert Kelso Cassatt, 1885

100 × 81.2cm, Philadelphia Museum of Art

Cassatt had made several attempts at a portrait of her favourite brother, Alexander (or 'Aleck'), before this one, but neither she nor her family had considered them successful. Alexander and his youngest son, Robbie, arrived in Paris on Christmas Day 1884, to visit Mrs Cassatt, who had been ill, and to enable Alexander to do business in Europe. They stayed for several months, during which time they sat for this double portrait.

This study of paternity provides an interesting contrast to the paintings of mothers and their children which Cassatt produced later, in particular that of Louisine Havemeyer and her daughter Electra, of 1895. The former is a tightly controlled picture of high contrasts of black formal clothes and light curtains and upholstery; the latter a looser, relaxed pose with the models gently smiling. Alexander and Robbie appear soberly dignified, and the position of the little boy's hands contribute to the calm, deliberate air of the portrait. The father, as befits an extremely successful man of business, seems to let his gaze stray to the paper at his knee.

As we shall come to expect of Cassatt's parent and child pieces, she creates within a distinctive abstract surface design (here made blatant by the colouring) a feeling of great tenderness through the placement of heads and hands. The formal pattern of vertical and horizontal created by the boy's legs and his father's straight left arm is balanced by the very loose handling of the familiar flowered armchair from the Cassatt apartment, and by the clear-complexioned faces.

Alexander had already written that 'Mary was a great favorite of mine, I suppose because our tastes were a good deal alike' – especially in matters of horse-riding. Little Robert was hailed by the family as the next Cassatt to be an artist, and Mary instructed him on the correct practice in her letters. To his older brother, Eddie, she had written in January 1881: 'I want you to tell Rob from me that when he gets his paint box he must promise to draw carefully a portrait of one of you, beginning with the eyes (remember) & send it to Grandmother.' While Cassatt's portraits are often marked by a distance from her sitters, here she subtly indicates not only the remarkable closeness of father and son and the similarity of their gaze, but also the affection of a sister and aunt.

The Sisters, c. 1885

46.2 × 56cm, Glasgow Art Gallery and Museum

After Cassatt's death in 1926, the *New York Herald Tribune* published an editorial obituary containing the following perceptive appraisal: 'It is an amusing paradox in her history that her force, her penetrating vision, her technical dexterity, were wreaked largely upon the most fragile of themes.'

The oil-sketch demonstrates Cassatt's strengths employed with characteristic control. In an American private collection there exists a less finished version which establishes the study's main features, its colouring and its high viewpoint. This latter serves to emphasize the smallness of the little girls, making them look upward with wide-eyed uncertainty. Cassatt frequently used this device to create interesting compositional angles and to force figures together, as in *The Bath* (see p. 107); here, the older girl casts a protective arm around her sister – the poignancy of the gesture reinforced by the onlooker's looming viewpoint.

The robust manipulation of long, thick strokes of green paint to block in the background area does not overpower the delicate expressiveness of the sitters' faces: Cassatt's free Impressionist touch was still sure, although by this date she was moving towards a greater concentration on untroubled planes of colour to match her solid compositions.

Mary Cassatt

Mr Robert S. Cassatt on Horseback, 1885

91.5 × 71cm, Adelson Galleries, Inc., New York

During 1884, Cassatt's productivity was severely curtailed by the need to care for her mother, who was in poor health, and by time-consuming arrangements to move the household to a new address in Paris. During trying periods such as this, Cassatt's relationship with her father showed signs of strain, as their strong personalities clashed. Like Mary herself in later life, Mr Cassatt was becoming increasingly irascible, although he had come to support her career and wrote of her achievements with pride. Nevertheless, this picture shows him in a happier light, as Cassatt began to pick up her work again in 1885.

The whole Cassatt family had a direct interest in horse-racing, an aristocratic enthusiasm shared with Degas. The household always had at least one horse, and Mary herself was an expert horsewoman, although she suffered at least two dangerous accidents while riding or driving in France.

Of this picture, Mary wrote to Alexander in September 1885: 'We are getting on much as usual here, I must work again and have done a large pastel of Father on Isabelle with which he is much delighted, but he says you will never believe that she is as handsome as I have made her . . . She has been the delight of Father all summer as he has done most of the riding when I was ill . . . '

The personal significance of this picture makes its unrevealing viewpoint puzzling. Mr Cassatt was a notoriously unhelpful model, falling asleep during portrait sessions, and the artist may have been forced to adopt this 'realistically' awkward angle to compensate for his lack of concentration. Alternatively, the stance may symbolize the distance she sometimes wished to place between her father and herself.

Young Woman Working in a Garden (Femme Cousante), c. 1886

91.5 × 64.7cm, Musée D'Orsay, Paris

This charming study, which Cassatt exhibited at the eighth Impressionist exhibition, bears witness to her development through Impressionist *plein air* interests to her mature classical style, with its firmer modelling and composition. In 1880 she had painted her sister crocheting in a similar flower-filled garden at Marly-le-Roi. Two drypoint sketches, which Adelyn Breeskin dates from around 1883, indicate that the sitter shown here may have been Susan, the maid (see pp. 21, 75). In both prints a female figure is placed against an *allée* of tree trunks, which find their compositional equivalent in the painting in the steeply-angled garden path. In one print the same model's full lips and high lace collar are recognizable; in the other, her head is lowered in concentration as she examines something held in her raised hands. The long delicate drypoint lines in which Cassatt suggests the strong lighting contrasts of the open air are paralleled in the sweeping brushstrokes which animate the shadows in the top left of the painting.

By the mid 1880s, Cassatt was contrasting this energetic treatment of peripherals with a disciplined concentration on the compactness of her central figures. Susan's head and arms form a quiet focus, reinforced by the frame of the chair back, within the larger triangle of her pale blue dress. The use of a characteristically high viewpoint underscores the sitter's complete self-absorption. She holds our attention despite the exuberant diagonal sweep of the path and the brilliant red of the surrounding geraniums.

Girl Arranging Her Hair, 1886

75.5 × 62.2cm, National Gallery of Art, Washington, DC

This picture was much admired by Degas, who kept it in his private collection until his death in 1917. When it was discovered in his studio during the settling of his estate, it was at first thought to have been his own work. Considering the high esteem in which Cassatt had always held Degas, this case of mistaken identity must have been a source of great pride. The same picture had elicited from Degas some rare, unqualified praise, an event whose background was related by Achille Segard:

> 'The story is that one day, in front of Degas, Miss Cassatt in assessing a well known painter of their acquaintance dared to say: "He lacks style." At which Degas began to laugh, shrugging his shoulders as if to say: These meddling women who set themselves up as judges! What do they know about style?.
>
> 'This made Miss Cassatt angry. She want out and engaged a model who was extremely ugly, a servant-type of the most vulgar kind. She had her pose in a robe next to her dressing-table, with her left hand at the nape of her neck holding her meagre tresses while she combed them with her right, in the manner of a woman preparing for bed. The model is seen almost entirely in profile. Her mouth hangs open. Her expression is weary and stupid.
>
> 'When Degas saw the painting, he wrote to Miss Cassatt: What drawing! What style!'

Segard makes Cassatt's argument appear cruder than was the case. Her point was that, like Degas, Manet and Van Gogh, she was experimenting with 'ugly' subjects which could be transfigured by colouring, drawing and composition – in short, by artistic style – to create images which were beautiful because true. She declared her preference for 'health and strength' in her models, and this picture ironically reverses the usual associations of the toilette subject, linking it to natural simplicity rather than to beauty and vanity. It was natural for Degas to appreciate and secure a painting which shared his own interest in and treatment of these themes: Cassatt wrote that it was Degas who had first pointed out to her that Botticelli's love of truth extended to his painting the Virgin herself with fingernails worn down by field work.

The Letter, 1890–1

34.5 × 21.1cm, The Metropolitan Museum of Art, New York

Surprisingly, this is the only picture on the theme of correspondence that Cassatt attempted. Cassatt was an habitual letter-writer: to her family and friends in Philadelphia, to her artist colleagues in France and to all those to whom she entrusted her professional and domestic affairs. Even in later life, when her eyesight was failing, she continued to write her correspondence herself, determined to retain this means of expression when the comfort of family and art were denied her (see p. 38). It has been suggested that the compulsory grind of all her correspondence dulled Cassatt's interest in the romantic overtones and traditions attached to letter-writing, hence her neglect of the subject. Nevertheless, she would have seen many examples of the subject of women reading letters in the Japanese woodcuts which originally inspired her own prints, and the sensual implications of these original pictures of courtesans and love-letters are perhaps in evidence in Cassatt's own composition – in the contemplative sealing of the envelope, indicating concealment – though in a more reticent manner to match the class of discreet young lady which peopled Cassatt's works.

In this colour print she produces a perfect example of the 'atmospheric' effects, rather than mere technical duplication of images, at which she was aiming in most of the 'Set of Ten' series of prints. Her debt to the exhibition of Japanese prints which so enthralled her and many other avant-garde artists in the spring of 1890 is particularly evident here. Indeed, the borrowings are so clear as to suggest that the picture, despite its respectable Western theme, was conceived as a self-conscious tribute to Oriental modes. Above all the effect is highly decorative in its juxtaposition of intricate pattern and abstract flat forms. The desk top is distorted in contravention of conventional perspective as recognized by Western art, while even more noticeable is the different treatment of the face and hands from that seen in the other prints, with the exception of the baby in *The Bath*. The girl's fingers curl around the envelope in the same way that they grip the samisen in the illustration on p. 29, while her slightly cross-eyed gaze marks her as a beauty in traditional Japanese style. Cassatt's command of these alien cultural elements was so confident that the resulting image is one of her most enduring and satisfying creations.

Mary Cassatt

The Dress Fitting, 1890–1

37.7 × 25.6cm, The Metropolitan Museum of Art, New York

In this colour print Cassatt concentrated on the subtle effects that could be obtained with a range of closely allied colours and juxtaposed patterns. The subject was also new for her, dealing as it did both with a female activity beyond the home and with communication between different social classes. In this expansion of thematic interest, Cassatt appears to have been deliberately preparing herself for the wider symbolism of the Chicago mural project, in which the same model (also seen in *The Lamp* and *Afternoon Tea Party*) is central.

Only one drawing related to this print survives, although it does not appear to have been used to transfer the final design, which has led to the suggestion that the lines were drawn freely on to the plate. A more revealing relationship can be traced within the painting *Woman Holding a Red Zinnia*, in which the model wears the same dress, with its distinctive bodice, for what she is being fitted in the print. Cassatt's interest in fashion led to one critic of the mural project describing its theme as 'modern woman glorified by Worth' (the noted couturier). Whether that was justified or not, here we see the most explicit treatment of a subject which was close to Cassatt's heart.

While the finished composition has a delicate certainty to it, there is evidence of a readjustment of the angle of the standing model's head between the first and second state, on the first plate containing the drypoint outlines. The new pose suggests the slightly awkward anxiety of the client keen to be well dressed, standing stiffly while the seamstress makes her alterations. Cassatt wished to capture in drypoint the nuances of expression which she could obtain through any other medium, and burnishing away mistaken lines allowed her to be exacting.

The large-scale organization of the picture is as carefully executed as its detail, with the high viewpoint allowing for the steep rake of the wall to give interest, and the dark form of the crouching woman creating a supportive base for the figure group. The finest of lines in the hair of both women, and in the sleeve of the new dress, are played off against wide planes of colour and pattern – in particular the heavy stripes of the seamstress's dress and the arabesques on the carpet. Once again, Cassatt absorbs the formal characteristics of Japanese prints into a modern scene and, in addition, plays on a further facet of the contemporary craze for '*Japonisme*'. Many of the *ukiyo-e* print themes were excuses to depict particularly elaborate kimonos; Monet's full-length portrait of his wife, of 1875–6, adopted and adapted this characteristic. In this print, dress is the pretext for, but is the *least* detailed part of, the print.

Afternoon Tea Party, 1890–1

34.8 × 26.3cm, The Metropolitan Museum of Art, New York

There are no contemporary paintings, prints or pastels directly related to this print, but in it Cassatt was renewing her acquaintance with a theme which had been successfully received in earlier works such as *Five o'Clock Tea* (p. 12). Again, this is a specifically female scene, part of the social round of the bourgeois woman, although 'afternoon tea' could also provide a point of contact for less conventional souls. Cassatt is known to have held 'At Homes' for the increasing number of female American art students, like May Alcott, who were following her to Paris, attracted by her avant-garde reputation. Cassatt enjoyed good conversation, and dispensed valuable advice to her visitors at these afternoon gatherings. This print combines the acceptably feminine with the practical and forceful artistic personality which Cassatt herself could embody.

We have already seen how Cassatt preserved in her pictures favourite objects, often china, from her Paris apartment – a reflection of her role as proud householder. This print unusually includes gold touches on the rims of the teacups, painted on after printing. These details were evidently important to the success of the picture, although the print is not cluttered with objects. The edition contained several colour variations, mostly affecting the tablecloth and the hostess' dress, and Cassatt subtly manipulated her image to suggest a light-filled, genteel atmosphere. The delicate arms and hands unite the two halves of the composition, the muted tones of the right-hand side balancing the warmer, heavier colouring around the somewhat formidable figure of the visitor. The hostess has the submissive air and pose of an acolyte in this domestic ritual, and Cassatt altered the facial expressions of the figures between the fourth and the fifth and final states, removing the visitor's smile. She may have been aiming at the solemn mood of some Japanese prints, which often featured tea and other ceremonies. Ironically, here the hostess' respectability is being tested; the Oriental models, with their elegant geisha girls and tea-house settings, were concerned with very different criteria.

Mary Cassatt

Woman Bathing, 1890–1

37.1 × 27cm, Worcester Art Museum

A very rare treatment of a female nude subject, this is one of Cassatt's purest figure drawings, derived in great part from the work of the Japanese artists who had so impressed her at the 1890 exhibition. The volume of the arms and trunk is suggested entirely by their boundary lines, in the manner of Utamaro, Nishikawa Sokenobu or Kosotei Toyokuni, who depicted similar subjects – often in black and white alone, which served to emphasize their precision and simplicity of line. Cassatt's other well-known nude, *The Coiffure*, also appeared in the 'Set of Ten', and it is interesting to note that she treats these traditionally sensual subjects as vehicles for the study of line rather than the nuances of shading and texture that flesh-painting generally receives.

The influence of Degas, who had been producing his 'bathers' series for about a decade, is evident here. His *The Washbasin* could be a model for Cassatt's piece. Again, as in *Girl Arranging Her Hair*, Cassatt aimed to prove to him that talent was not a function of sex. Segard described the woman's back in this print thus: 'It is traced with a single stroke and yet it is round and firm. It turns as naturally as do the soft backs of young women. In front of this print, Degas had said, "This back, did you draw this?" ' The deep impression that this print made on Degas may have been reflected in his announcement, made just after the exhibition of the 'Set of Ten' in summer 1891, that he intended 'to do a suite of lithographs, a first series on nude women at their toilette . . . ' However, Degas never attempted colour printing, and he was never engaged by such direct imitation of oriental techniques and effects.

Cassatt has used three of the properties which appear in another bathing scene (see p. 107) – the distinctively striped dress, the china jug and the basin. The figure itself receives less emphasis in terms of pattern and colour: it is the beautiful line of the back and the description of the elbow and wrist which attract the eye and admiration, with the curve of the jug serving as a reinforcing echo. Here, Cassatt pays a suitably veiled tribute to the sensuality, even eroticism, which attracted the Parisian art world to the world of eighteenth-century Japan.

Detail is balanced by large areas of flat colour in the wall and the dresser, which is paradoxically both three-dimensional by virtue of its drawing and completely flattened by the application of brown ink. However, Cassatt also produces a range of colour effects within the basic blue, pink and green chosen – especially on the wall and the boldly patterned carpet – by remixing the ink between printings. The pattern of the carpet itself appears to exceed its purely representational function and begins to take on a decorative power hinting at effects achieved by Matisse in the next century.

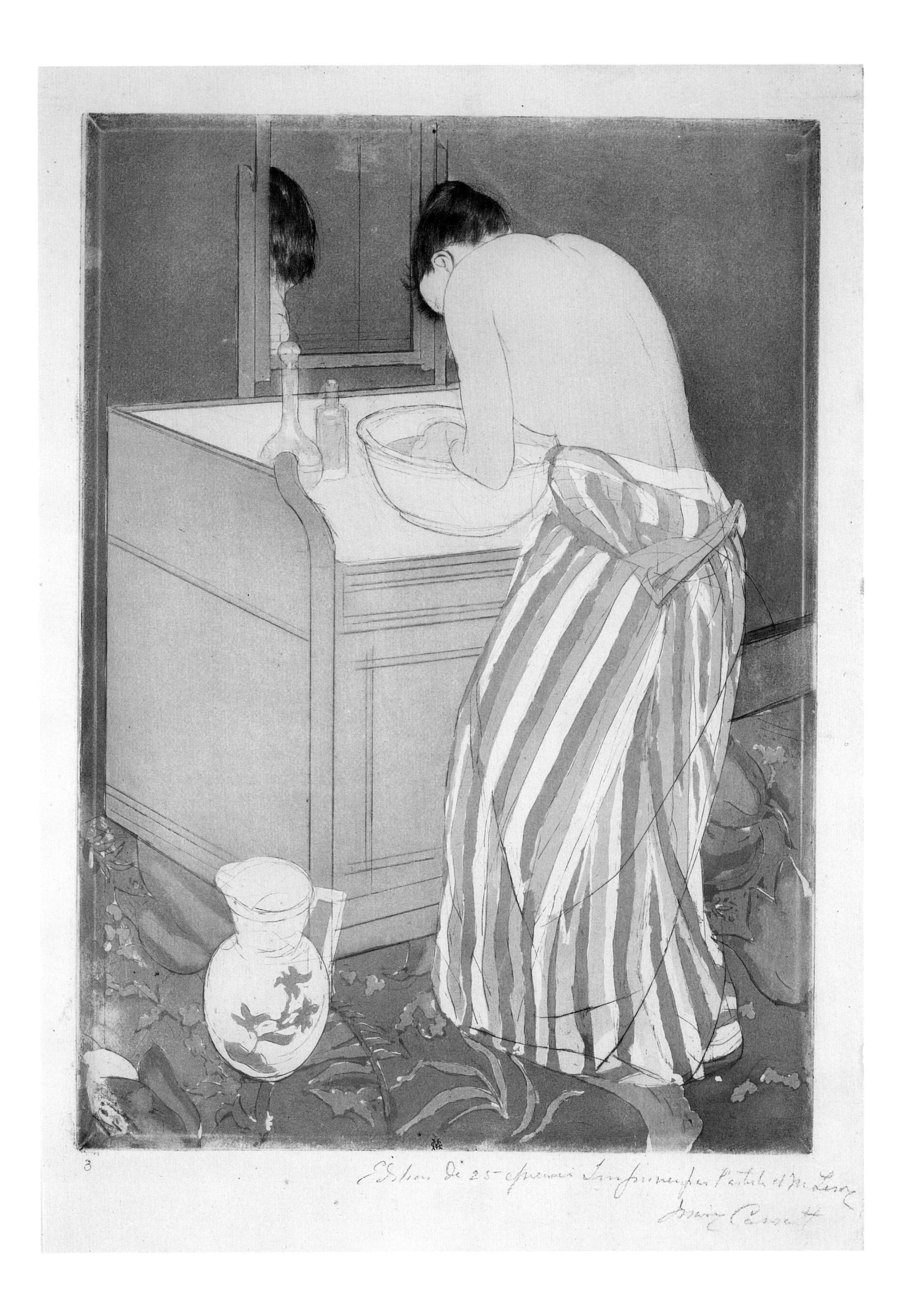

In the Omnibus, 1890–1

38.4 × 26.7cm, Boston Public Library, Print Department

We know a good deal about Cassatt's processes of refining her colour print compositions, both from the various extant impressions taken from each plate (usually three) and from her preparatory drawings. In this case, these show her following what was, for her, an unusual course in altering the content of the picture between the drawing and the first state. She was in the habit of using the drawing simply to transfer a worked-out design on to the plate, here using a soft-ground method. A metal plate coated with a waxy ground is covered with the paper bearing the design. When this is traced over with a sharp point and the paper is pulled away, the soft, acid-resistant ground is removed along the traced lines, which are then bitten with acid. However, the drawing for *In the Omnibus* originally featured a seated male figure next to the mother and, superimposed over this, a less fully worked standing woman. Both were dropped from the final composition to concentrate on the charming group of young mother, child and maid.

This new technique had prompted Cassatt to develop a subject which truly belonged to the everyday lives of women of all classes, unlike the private garden or the drawing-room; however, she was not prepared to allow the common herd to share the carriage with her own characters. Interestingly, this was not a scruple shared by other artists of the day, including Madame J. Delance-Feurgard, whose print *Un Coin d'omnibus* was exhibited at the 1887 Salon. This shows a more realistically cramped, darkened space with a Parisian street visible through the window. Cassatt too opens up her usual narrow focus to include a view of the Seine and a bridge, but the effect here is of light and air. Alternative titles for the print include *Crossing a Bridge* and *En Bateau mouche*, and an acceptance of the latter may explain the somewhat stately atmosphere – not a normal bus ride but an afternoon boat-trip. This formality extends to the socially prescribed relationships of the characters: the elegant young mother is a spectator while the nurse attends to the child. Whatever its setting, this picture again displays Cassatt's compositional skills in the balance of abstract elements and delicately observed human features – the perfect framing of the mother's head against the river, and the extraordinary petal-like form of the baby's dress.

Mother's Kiss, 1890–1

38.4 × 26.7cm, Whittemore Collection, Library of Congress, Washington, DC

This was probably the second of the ten colour prints to be completed after *The Bath* (not shown), with which it shares certain antecedents and technical features. It is clearly related to the mother and child motifs which Cassatt had recently been working on in other media (see p. 105) and, like *The Bath*, shows a simple group of two figures with very little background interest. The rest of the 'Set of Ten' are distinguished by their more complex settings and means of production. These first two pictures were created using only two plates rather than three: in this case the first plate printed the outlines of hair and flesh in black and sanguine respectively, the dress pattern in drypoint and aquatint, and the olive-green and red aquatint of the chair, while the second plate printed the aquatint for the blue in the dress and the background. These blues vary subtly between different prints in the edition, and must surely have been in Pissarro's mind when he wrote praising Cassatt's achievements in aquatint to his son, Lucien: '. . . the tone even, subtle, delicate, without stains on seams: adorable blues, fresh rose, etc. Then what must we have to succeed? – money, yes, just a little money. We have to have copper plates, a *boîte à grain* [dusting box], this is a bit of a nuisance but it is absolutely necessary to have uniform and imperceptible grains and a good printer. But the result is admirable, as beautiful as Japanese work, and it's done with printer's ink! . . .'

The blue background here pays direct homage to the mica-dust backgrounds sometimes seen in the work of Utamaro; however, its subtlety is not a true reflection of Japanese colour as it would have appeared originally – the prints that Cassatt and her colleagues saw at the exhibition in 1890 were a century old, and had faded accordingly. The colours used by the French printmakers were more akin to those they favoured for their paintings, and Cassatt was careful to describe only *The Bath* as an attempt to imitate a Japanese work in specific details – in the remaining prints, the aim is more for 'atmosphere' and harmonizing colour.

Despite the clarity of this final state, evidence of its slightly tentative development is to be found below the baby's right foot and around the mother's head, where the lines of their original positions, incompletely burnished out of the plate, can still be seen. Cassatt integrates the vulnerable nakedness of the child into the sheltering silhouette of its mother – at one point the line of the mother's hand blends into the silhouette of the child's back, suggestive of a yielding continuity which reinforces the tender effectiveness of the theme. The artist's pictures of nude children demonstrates her ability to convey grace and vulnerability, here emphasized by the exquisite delicacy of the colouring.

Baby's First Caress, c. 1891

76.2 × 61cm, New Britain Museum of American Art, Connecticut

This fine pastel is closely related to the previous plate, depicting the same models in a similarly intimate way. We can recognize the woman's patterned dress and the plump child, and Cassatt again reduces the background to a plane of colour. However this picture is true to its own medium: the pastel strokes suggest textures – flesh, hair and cloth – whereas the print focused on the virtuoso drawing of the joint silhouette, modelling with line. Here, the baby's plumpness is expressed with a subtlety of colour-blending akin to the shading in the drypoint *Baby's Back*, produced at around the same time (see p. 24).

Despite the opening out of the group, the intimate mood is preserved in the child's gesture and by the mother's left hand as it supports his tiny foot. In works like this, Cassatt was especially skilful in her deployment of touching, interlinking hands to create a sense of mutual trust and love. She was careful to insist on the secular and domestic spirituality of these pictures, but they also reflect the simplicity and frontality of the religious pictures she studied in Parma. Art historian Anna Jameson's famous work *Legends of the Madonna as Represented in the Fine Arts*, first published in 1852, presented multiple images of the Madonna and Child in variations strongly reminiscent of Cassatt's compositions.

The theme of maternity was in vogue among many European artists around this time, and was increasingly popular in the United States. Cassatt's abiding interest in it may have stemmed as much from her desire to open up America to her work as from aesthetic ambitions, and it was also natural for her, as an associate of the Impressionists, to treat a subject in series. However, her career has been linked ever since with these sympathetic pictures, and several are among her most characteristic productions, displaying all her clarity of vision, sensitive drawing and emotional truthfulness.

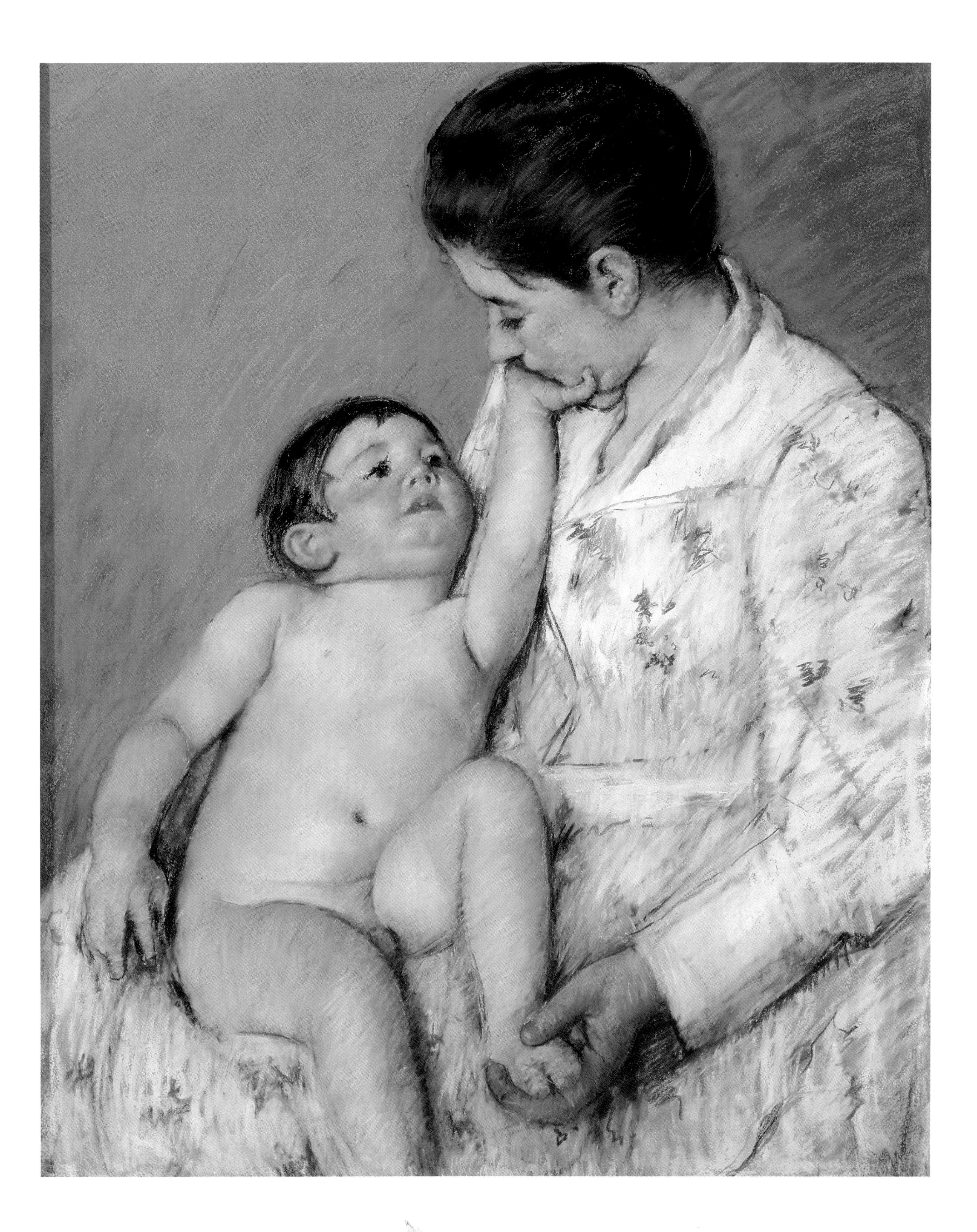

The Bath, c. 1891

100.3 × 66cm, The Art Institute of Chicago

This picture received a good deal of attention at the various museum shows at which it was exhibited during the artist's lifetime, firstly in Paris in 1893, where it was found evidence of Cassatt's 'lively sentiment, exquisite taste, and great talent.'

Unusually for this stage in her career, she uses a slightly older child, but she retains the extreme refinement of feeling that characterizes her portraits of babies. Matched to this delicacy she deploys several of her characteristic compositional tactics to great effect, most strikingly the high viewpoint which, as in *The Sisters*, makes the figure group cohere as a single form, emphasizing the closeness of the two dark heads. The greater monumentality with which the figures are endowed through strategies such as this contributes to the dignified mood.

The influence of the Japanese print is still strong in the play with decorative patterns, in particular in the bottom half of the picture, where striped dress and carpet clash, and in the balancing of vertical and horizontal elements. Intimate feeling and decorative interest are held in a satisfying tension within the composition: the jug echoes both the effect of the child's white skin against the dark background and the curve of her left arm, while the strong vertical movements of the mother's arm and the child's legs, and their joint gaze into the washbowl, are reinforced by the wide stripes of the dress. Again, the mutual absorption of the couple finds expression in the closeness of their hands and the parallel movement of limbs as the mother guides her uncertain child into the water. Caught up in their shared activity, the figures' faces are withdrawn from us, creating a moment of privacy which the spectator cannot violate.

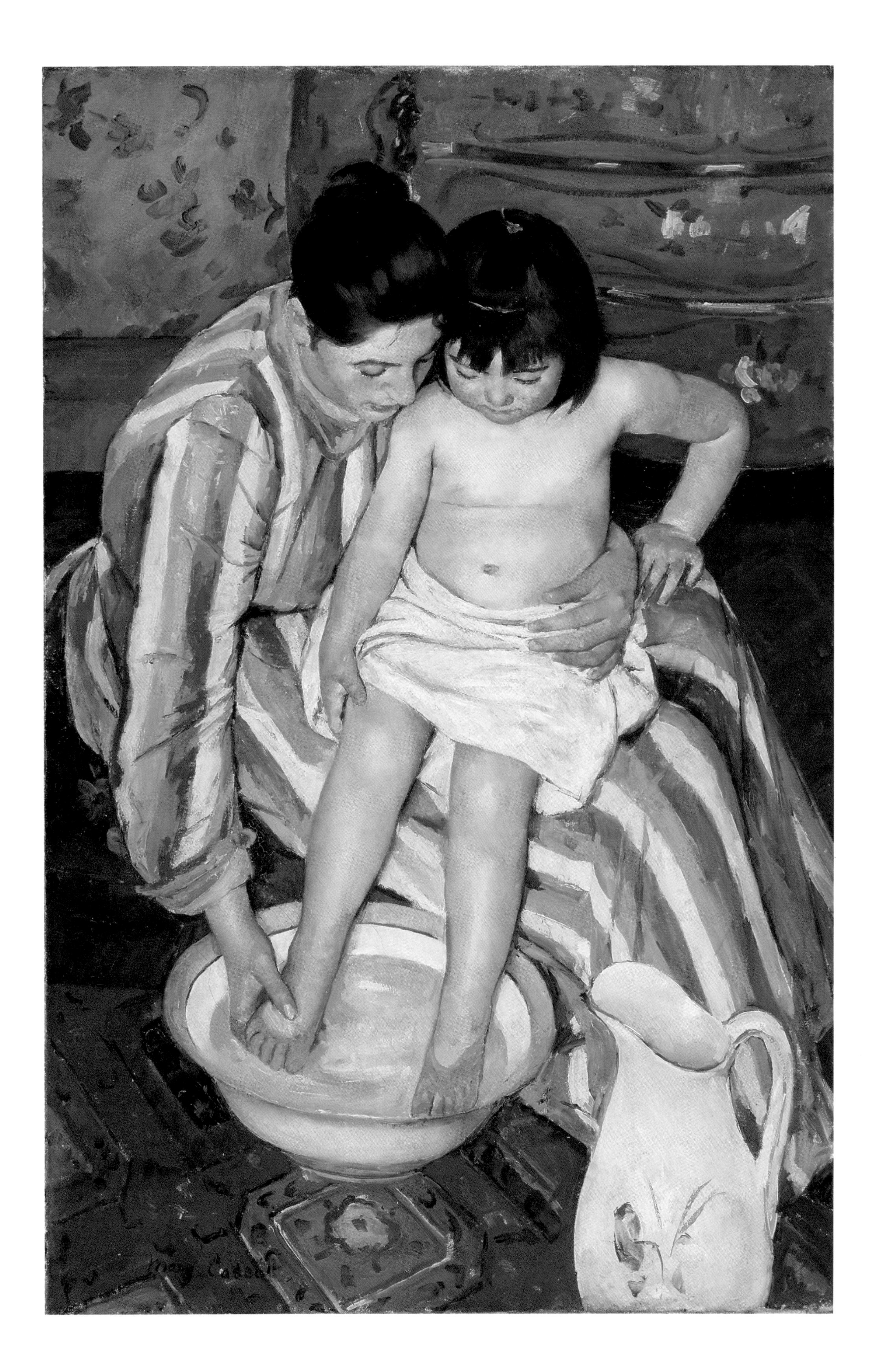
Mary Cassatt

The Family, c. 1892

81.2 × 66cm, Chrysler Museum, Norfolk, Virginia

By the late 1880s Cassatt had developed a very individual, though still flexible and open, artistic personality. The bright local colour and appeal to atmosphere of Impressionism was still sympathetic to her, but her devotion to figure subjects and her determination to improve her draughtsmanship made her pictures of the late 1880s focus on precise delineation and a more solid handling of paint surfaces. Around this time, too, she established her interest in the mother and child theme, which gave opportunities for painting flesh (Cassatt never showed interest in painting the female nude), for the expression of delicate female sentiments of which she approved and for the infusing of a modern scene with a modern spirituality.

Although Paul Durand-Ruel had hailed her as the painter of the modern Holy Family, Cassatt never attempted a specific Madonna subject, and certainly by the late nineteenth century it was almost impossible to dress sincere religious feeling in contemporary forms, as the Italian Renaissance masters had done. She declared that she could not believe in a personal God, although here the inspiration of the religious pictures she had so admired in Rome and Parma seems to have been her starting point. The triangular composition, the openly adoring female figures and the very specific symbolism of the carnation (like coral beads, grapes or pomegranates, a prefiguration of the Passion) featured in many Renaissance altarpieces. In Cassatt's picture, such elements are clearly derived from this great tradition of iconographic painting; the clear colours and the graceful mood may owe something to the contemporary revival of interest in the work of Botticelli. The open-air scene also gives this picture a curious significance, displacing the group from its expected, more confined setting of a nursery or private garden (in fact, the scenes which Cassatt would later paint) and universalizing it.

In spite of these throwbacks to earlier centuries, however, the picture is determinedly secular and contemporary, with much attention paid to details of dress, and with high-keyed colouring throughout. While Cassatt was later to suggest similar levels of feeling without resorting to such specific references to the spirituality of the past, it is perhaps the audacity of the comparisons she forces which here impress upon us the freshness of her vision, of the modern family still held together by love and trust.

Mary Cassatt

Gathering Fruit, c. 1893

42.2 × 29.8cm, The Metropolitan Museum of Art, New York

The mural project *Modern Woman* was most productive for Cassatt, in terms of the many related works it inspired. At least nine of these, delivered to Durand-Ruel while Cassatt worked on the mural during 1892 and 1893, were exhibited at the large show of her work at the dealer's at the end of 1893. She herself acknowledge that the mural themes offered a rich source of images, especially for prints, although this and *The Banjo Lesson* were the only prints known to have been completed, and a projected series was never made. However, this print was used to develop the larger-scale painting *Baby Reaching for an Apple*, with which it shares similarities of pose and symbolism.

The print is unusual in the existence of a preliminary coloured drawing, although no early states with hand colouring remain. Cassatt experimented with both the drypoint outlines and the aquatint colours, taking the print through eleven states. Some of these intermediate states were exhibited with the final version in 1893, as Cassatt had come to regard the process and the results of printmaking as of equal artistic validity and interest, the former illuminating the issues and choices which had faced the artist. The final composition is a remarkably skilful union of surface pattern with the creation of deep space to the right, where we look through the garden doorway to a distant sundial. Again, Cassatt characteristically creates strong vertical elements, using the figures, doorway and ladder, which are then counterbalanced by the diagonal linking of the arms and the horizontal patterns of the rungs and bricks. As in *Woman Bathing*, the subtle combination of green and rose owes much to Japanese art – or at least to the faded colour of the century-old woodcuts seen by their Parisian admirers.

It has been suggested that Cassatt was attempting more than the depiction of modern life here, and we may expect some deeper symbolism from a work connected with her dignified representation of *Modern Woman*. Although we see an espaliered pear-tree, the woman offers the baby a bunch of grapes and, on closer inspection, vine leaves appear. The grape has obvious sacramental associations, while the view beyond the wall is a distant reminder of time passing, of harvests ending. These possibilities are given credibility by the strength and deliberation of the figures, but the overall and immediate impression is, probably as the artist intended, of a warm, sun-filled garden where no darker presence threatens.

Mary Cassatt

Baby Reaching for an Apple, 1893

100.3 × 65.4cm, Virginia Museum of Fine Arts, Richmond

As we have seen, this picture was closely related to a group of works inspired by the Chicago mural. It was probably one of the last to be completed, being based on the preceding plate and at a further remove from the original composition. The single mother with her child harks back to Cassatt's simple maternal scenes of the late 1880s, while retaining something of the air of symbolic ritual which permeates the mural.

A new daring in the treatment of figures is to be seen in the startling juxtaposition of the heads of the woman and baby. The three visible eyes are an even more graphic indication of united purpose and feeling than attempted previously in her work. Nancy Mowll Mathews has pointed to a possible source for this device, again illustrated in Anna Jameson's *Legends of the Madonna as Represented in the Fine Arts*: here, a drawing, of an Albrecht Dürer Madonna and Child in which the artist also cuts off the view of the Mother's face, held close behind that of the Child, in what Jameson had classified as the most intimate type of representation of the subject. Whatever her sources for the figure group, Cassatt refers to the past to make more specific the symbolism of gathering and distributing fruit which she had deployed in the mural. In many Renaissance Madonna and Child compositions, the Virgin holds out to her Son a stem of grapes or a pomegranate, which foreshadow his Passion. Cassatt's women likewise guide future generations to their destinies.

The colours are stronger versions of those in the print, applied with an eye to the outlines of the dress and the fruit and skilfully detaching the heads from the complex patterns covering the upper section of the canvas. In this, and in its narrow vertical format, the painting has overtones of Japanese art, while the interlacing of the branches and the interplay of the arms and hands are used to develop some sense of space and movement around the surface.

In the Garden, 1893

73 × 60cm, Baltimore Museum of Art

Flowers were always a favourite element in Cassatt's work, usually contained in garden borders, vases or fabric patterns. Here they spill out over most of the surface, to create an overall decorative effect, indicating another tradition in which Cassatt took an interest around this time – she had begun to collect Persian miniatures, possibly under the influence of Henry Havemeyer, who had been an enthusiast of eastern art for many years. The delicate decorative pattern in such pieces is reflected in *In the Garden*, where the figures are seen against a wall of plant forms which both suggests the colour and shade of the vegetation and acts as a flat backdrop. The presence of partially indicated flowers on the woman's dress and on the child's smock links foreground and background, allowing us to see the picture in two ways: as representative of figures in a garden and as a flat design in which wide black and white shapes and the more fragmented floral pattern are bound together by the broad application of pastel in long but precisely aimed strokes of colour. Only the faces and to some extent the arms are given a more detailed treatment, with shorter blended strokes.

Cassatt claimed to have no admiration for artists of a later school whom she believed were misguided in their experiments with primitive forms and abstraction. However, this picture appears to have very specific links to Post-Impressionist tendencies, such as those of the young Nabis like Édouard Vuillard, or even of individuals like Odilon Redon, whose deployment of floating, spatially indeterminate flowers within the traditional portrait form Cassatt anticipates here.

As in so many of Cassatt's pictures of maternity, the composition and mood are almost hieratic, presenting the child as the focus of veneration for both the mother and the onlooker. Despite the covert references to Renaissance iconography, however, Cassatt's is a determinedly modern vision, which fills this atmospheric piece with the light of the unseen sun.

Mary Cassatt

The Boating Party, 1894

90.2 × 117.1cm, National Gallery of Art, Washington, DC

This picture was the centre-piece of Cassatt's first solo show in the United States, held at Durand-Ruel's New York galleries in 1895. It remains unusual within her body of work for its colouring, complex composition and subject-matter, and it may be seen as a further development shaped by her work for the Chicago mural and the 'Set of Ten' print series. From 1893 Cassatt spent several summers on the Mediterranean coast at Antibes, where she was stirred to experiment with harder, decorative colour, and where the *plein air* subjects expected of Impressionism came readily to hand. Particular attention has been paid to the abstract shapes created by the sail and the foreshortened boat, indicating a continued fascination with the decorative coloured planes of Japanese art, while the introduction of a male character into her usual cast of young women and children suggests that Cassatt was striving for new psychological as well as compositional effects.

Whereas in her pictures of mothers, children or sisters our expectations of the relationships depicted are clearly defined and answered, here there is ambiguity and mystery. The man's form acts as a repoussoir figure to direct our eye, but also confounds our expectations of a Cassatt work. Placed in the foreground, his black-clad back closes off one side of the picture, while his braced left arm points into its centre and focuses our attention on the more colourful woman and child. Despite this guidance, a reading of the whole picture is complicated by the exchange of glances which animates it. The central figures have something of the self-absorbed expression familiar from other works on the theme of mothers and children, and this reinforces their close relationship, as does the integrity of their outline which detaches them from the background of sea and from the man. They are physically separated from him by the transom seat in the boat, as well as through colour, and his strenuous energy is contrasted to their passivity and calm. An impression of divergence rather than unity is also suggested by the oar and by the arcing sail which counterbalances the expanse of black on the right. At the same time, however, there appears to be some indefinable communication between the three, the squirming child in particular acting with reassuring normality, although we cannot identify the man as either father or boatman. Despite the many tensions within the picture, its compositional and emotional effectiveness is undiminished. Cassatt herself seems to have regarded the work favourably, for she kept it in her own collection for many years – at least until 1914.

Summertime, 1894

73.7 × 96.5cm, Armand Hammer Foundation, Los Angeles

Though related to *The Boating Party* in its theme and in the increasing freedom of Cassatt's oil technique at this time, *Summertime* has none of that picture's ambiguities. It marks a return to her first embracing of Impressionist interests around the 1880s and can be related to works by Monet, such as *The Boat at Giverny* of 1887, in its concentration on everyday themes and the effects of light on varied surfaces. Despite the vivid sheen of the water and the bustle of the ducks, Cassatt creates again the quiet, contemplative mood which she saw as appropriate to scenes of female companionship.

Paradoxically, she achieved this mood using much looser brushwork, which may have developed in parallel with her increased interest in pastel work, which also deployed areas of bright colour in small patches or brief strokes to catch subtle highlights or to suggest movement. Cassatt also attempted to capture the atmosphere of the same scene in a later colour print, *Feeding the Ducks* of 1895. This is also related to an oil-sketch, *On the Water*, which has the same sunlit atmosphere, though without the brilliant tonal contrasts suggestive of high summer which we enjoy here. Cassatt had realized the value of working through her motifs in varied media, especially after the fruitful exploration of themes inspired by the *Modern Woman* mural. In this instance, while the print has a delicate quality, it is in *Summertime* that the subject is rendered with the greatest spirit and success.

Portrait of Mrs H.O. Havemeyer, 1896

73.6 × 61cm, Shelburne Museum, Shelburne, Vermont

Friendship features in several of Cassatt's works of the mid-1890s, most personally in this portrait of Louisine Elder Havemeyer, who had been her staunch ally since their first meeting in Paris in 1874. In 1883, Louisine married Henry O. Havemeyer, the 'Sugar King' and himself a collector of oriental objects and Barbizon-school paintings. Both were willing recipients of Cassatt's advice on all matters related to the enhancement of their magnificent art collection – from what to buy to how it should best be transported. Cassatt's aim to improve the state of her country's cultural resources as an aid to future American artists was realized through the Havemeyers' seemingly inexhaustable funds, and they in turn were able to bequeath to the Metropolitan Museum in New York over a thousand of their unparalleled collection of works by the Impressionists and the earlier masters who had inspired them. Cassatt gave up valuable time to accompany the Havemeyers on European tours, on the trail of works by Goya and El Greco, and her eye was almost unerring.

Louisine shared Cassatt's limitations as well as her enthusiasms – she too could not appreciate the art that superseded that of her own contemporaries, such as that by Matisse or Picasso, perhaps indicating the decisive power of the artist's influence.

Despite her position as a leader of American society Louisine allied herself to the causes of the exceptional, in particular that of women's suffrage, another interest to which Cassatt introduced her. Nevertheless, Cassatt depicts her here in the extravagant gown of a society matron, though the effect is direct rather than intimidating or formal. The pastel is worked most thoroughly around the face, suggesting heavily modelled features around a tolerant smile, although the pose of the hands suggest an impatience to be on the move.

The Conversation, c.1896

64.6 × 81.2cm, Private collection

In Impressionist art, women were often treated merely as decorative objects over which light falls, or as vehicles for displays of sensuous painting. The most influential figures for Cassatt in this area, as in so many others were Degas and Manet – particularly the former, whose pictures of women as dancers, *chanteuses*, prostitues and milliners show real people who inhabit and affect clearly defined worlds. As an artist whose mature work featured adult female figures and children almost exclusively, Cassatt needed a constantly updated repertoire of compositional ideas, and she drew on these examples to present female lives with emotional truth underpinning superficial appearances.

Cassatt's cast of female characters, however, were mothers, friends, sisters or solitary and self-possessed individuals cast not in altruistic or sexual roles but engaged in the everyday reading, sewing and writing which occupy ordinary lives. Many of her pictures convey a mood of contemplation and dignity, creating a distance between the observer and the observed, and the best of them force us to temper our appreciation of colour and texture with a recognition of the sitter as a distinct personality.

Like her *Portrait of Mrs H.O. Havemeyer*, Cassatt explores close friendship in this picture (it is subtitled *Two Sisters*). The opalescent pinks and blues of the fashionable dresses do not detract from the serious atmosphere of intense concentration which the girls generate, complementary mirror images of each other: one listening, one speaking. The psychological focus of the picture – the face of the girl to the right – is darker than much of its surroundings, shadowed by the figure of her sister to enhance the atmosphere of thoughtful quiet. Cassatt's continuing fascination with lighting effects fuses perfectly with the mood of the subject, while the changes in the handling of the pastel in different areas of the piece balance interest in technical means and psychological ends.

This picture was sold at auction for £2,402,770 ($4,510,000) at Christie's, New York, in 1988 – a record for a work by Cassatt and an indication of her status in the history of modern American art, which is now clearly not based solely on her claims to be the only major American or female Impressionist artist, but is an assessment of her on her own terms, as she would have wished.

Mother Combing Her Child's Hair, 1898

64 × 80cm, The Brooklyn Museum, New York

On her return from America in 1898, Cassatt completed this charming picture which proved indicative of the interests in child portraiture that were to dominate the next phase of her career. With her younger relatives now beyond her preferred age as models, she began to experiment with new faces and more complex compositions. Mother and baby subjects, although still included in her repertoire, gave way in part to larger family groupings and less generalized areas of activity. These older children were too much their own personalities to be contained within the passive roles Cassatt had assigned to her baby models: more specific activities were needed to occupy them in pictures such as this one. Indeed, a new dimension was added to their relationships, as the young girls in particular were now shown being initiated into the feminine rituals which Cassatt had portrayed with adult models. Susan Fillin-Yeh has noted that Cassatt's depictions of a traditional theme, the toilette, are quite often transferred to the lives of children, defusing its typical associations with the female nude while preserving the opportunities to capture a moment of innocent sensuality. Allied to this, the self-absorption of the couple makes *Mother Combing Her Child's Hair* especially touching – in particular the hands of both figures, expressive of tenderness, trust and patience.

Mother and Boy (The Oval Mirror), 1901

81.7 × 66cm, The Metropolitan Museum of Art, New York

One of the greatest of Cassatt's pictures of maternity, this painting of the model Antoinette earned some of the most unqualified praise the artist ever received from Degas, who declared it the finest painting of the century. However, he also dubbed it 'the infant Christ and his English nurse', and went on to define it as a painting which demonstrates 'all your qualities and all your faults'.

As in her pictures using younger children, Cassatt emphasizes the physical intimacy of the mother–child relationship, although in these later interpretations this unambiguous sensuality is a cause of greater unease. The painting earned a second title, *The Florentine Madonna*, although rather than resembling any Florentine work it is more reminiscent of the work of Parmigianino, one of Cassatt's key influences during her days in Parma, sharing something of the elegant and disturbing physical presence of that artist's madonnas. Though never mannered, Cassatt places a characteristic emphasis on a strong pattern of close heads and hands, and the flesh and the mother's robe are painted with solid, creamy tones.

The mirror here is used in a different way to its appearances in pictures of young women, or mothers and female children. Here it is neither an indicator of femininity nor a device to open up the space in which the figures are set, as in earlier pictures: instead, it is used to frame the boy's head like a halo – a deliberate effect emphasized in a drypoint sketch of the composition. In this way Cassatt demonstrates the demarcation of male and female roles which evidently appeared natural to her, and which is all-pervasive in her later mother and child subjects: male children, as here, are generally the focus of adoration (see for instance, *Jules Being Dried by his Mother*, or *Mother and Child* of 1914), while little girls are initiated into the activities and interests 'traditionally' allotted to them, such as sewing and grooming.

Cassatt's radicalism is embodied not in her subjects but in the confident composition and painterly technique which animate her best work. This thematic conservatism shaped her work, despite her advocacy of the 'modern note' in art, and of women's suffrage in politics. The Chicago mural may have depicted 'Young Girls Pursuing Fame', but Cassatt most successful art portrayed women in their domestic roles, symbols of nature and nurture.

Mary

Young Mother Sewing, 1902

92.3 × 73.7cm, The Metropolitan Museum of Art, New York

This picture, a bequest to the Metropolitan Museum from Louisine Havemeyer, represents the female half of the Cassatt vision of childhood, combining the familiar motifs of young women and mothers and children. The little girl neglectful of her domestic lesson is probably Margot (see p. 131).

As in the previous picture, the paint is treated in thick, sweeping strokes to give an overall effect of solid flesh, animated by white highlights on the clothes and the glowing orange flowers to the left. In two sketches for this picture, and a related drypoint, the pose of the child alters slightly, but the figure of the mother is treated consistently, with the most concentrated attention paid to the pattern of her striped dress. Cassatt's interest is as much in the formal qualities of the painting's surface pattern as in her models – they form a triangle of pale tones in the foreground, punctuated by the dark heads which catch the warmth of the flowers. The framing elements of the window counteract rather than accentuate the suggestion of deeper space in the woods outside, balancing the line of the wall and the rim of the cabinet while continuing the vertical movement of the figures. While a renewed interest in the works of the old masters had changed her handling of materials, with longer, freer strokes and thicker applications of colour, the overall tone is still pale and the concerns of the Japanese printmakers remain in evidence.

In progressing from sketches to this final composition, Cassatt brought the figures closer to the picture plane: the little girl is no longer seen full length, and there is a greater concentration on the faces. The two figures are unusual in that their attention is not focused internally, within their own relationship, as in *The Crochet Lesson* (see p. 139) and many other pictures. The little girl's gaze at the onlooker draws us into the picture, while her supporting right arm points up to her mother's delicately drawn hands and lowered eyes. Their softly delineated faces are touchingly expressive, and the familiar physical closeness is maintained.

Margot in Blue, 1902

61 × 50cm, The Walters Art Gallery, Baltimore

During her later years in residence at the Château de Beaufresne, Cassatt continued her habit of using her family, household and any compliant neighbours as models. Among these were the children of the villagers, several of whom appear repeatedly in portrait series. These pictures (even in an unfinished state) were among the most popular the artist ever produced, and she fully intended them to be exhibited and sold to the public, rather than producing them as specific commissions from the sitters' families. Demand was great, and Vollard, in particular, persuaded her to release for sale sketches which she would not normally have preserved, let alone allowed to leave the studio. They combine her usual sensitive treatment of the features, the suggestion of soft skin and sweet natures, with a robust use of pastel in the backgrounds, to some extent avoiding the cloying sentimentality inherent in this kind of theme. Oils of the same period were not always as successful in balancing bland subject-matter with adventurous technique.

Pictures like *Margot in Blue* advanced her reputation among the critics as well as the public, with supporters of Impressionism such as Gustave Geffroy hailing her as the finest child-portraitist of her time. Cassatt's changed use of child subjects, from the context of the mother–child relationship to uncomfortable isolation in adult clothes, in part reflected the new century's interest in child psychology. Always alert, if not sympathetic, to the intellectual issues of her day, Cassatt could not have been ignorant of this current. It would be too crude an analysis to suggest that these child portraits were a conscious attempt to fill the absence of a family of her own, yet the subject evidently attracted her strongly. However, the repetitive, impersonal treatment and the systematic variation of colour schemes (little Margot also appears in white, orange and red) indicate that Cassatt, even at this late stage in a successful career, was still more intent on perfecting her pastel technique and exploring colour effects. While extremely accomplished and often touching, these pictures lack the emotional content of her mother and child groups – the artist seems somewhat detached from her sitters, whose natural delicacy is mocked by their fussy, outsize clothes, At the same time, the distinctive use of fashion in these pictures reflects Cassatt's abiding love of clothes – which extended to hats like the Riboux creation she wears in the photograph on p. 39. Here the hat is used to create a natural frame for the face, emphasizing the doll-like diminutiveness of her subject.

Mary Cassatt

Mother and Child, c. 1905

92.1 × 73.3cm, National Gallery of Art, Washington, DC

Here we see Cassatt reusing a setting and a colour scheme, as she did habitually throughout her career. Although relatively liberated by money, connections and ambition, women artists like Cassatt and Berthe Morisot were still limited in their choice of subjects by social conventions which, for instance, shut them out of such Impressionist meeting-places as the Café Guerbois. They had therefore to exercise considerable ingenuity in constantly finding new contexts and compositions within the largely domestic sphere available to them.

The earlier *Mother Combing her Child's Hair* (p. 125) shows the same corner of a room, probably in Cassatt's Château de Beaufresne. (The plate opposite also has a paired picture showing a different model in the same sunflower-adorned dress.) An even more complex and pointed use is made of the mirror in this later treatment, although at first it is still a device to drive space back from the picture plane, counteracting the flattening effect of the smoothly applied brown of the wall. However, the attention of the mother and child soon directs us to the focus of the picture, the glass in which we see the little girl reflected, just as her mother's profile can be seen in the wall mirror.

Despite not having children of her own, and her concentration on her career, she still emphasizes the maternal role as an educative one, where education consists of transmitting traditionally agreed roles to the next generation. These roles are determined by class as well as by sex – wealthier ladies initiate their daughters into the leisured rituals of beauty, while more modest women teach practical skills like sewing and crochet. Here such issues are made less explicit by the use of bright, unreal colours and costume.

The pose of the figures contributes an atmosphere of allegory: the female child is being introduced to a symbol of vanity, a trait traditionally associated with womankind. The unexplained sunflower also causes us to question its possible significance. The figures are further from the picture surface than in earlier pictures and are therefore shown more fully, to form a monumental triangular group. However, the application of the colour flattens out this potentially imposing effect, and the green frames of the chair and mirror reassert themselves as patterning or abstract elements.

mary cassatt

Mother and Two Children, 1905

100.5cm diameter, Westmoreland County Museum of Art

Cassatt's later career was deeply involved with the artistic life of her own country, although she did not return there after 1908. While the greater part of this involvement centred on helping her wealthy American associates build fine collections of European art, in 1905 she again attempted a public art project. The competition for decorations for the Women's Lounge at the Statehouse in Harrisburg, Pennsylvania, was especially appealing, in its proximity to Cassatt's birthplace, in the challenge of a tondo form and in the appropriateness of the theme to her own favoured motifs. Unfortunately, the project proved a disappointment in several respects.

Cassatt completed two of the tondi before learning that the building project for which they were intended was riddled with corruption. She then withdrew from the competition. She kept the two pictures in her personal collection, with the intention of giving them to her nephews and nieces, but as the years passed she appears to have become distanced from them, especially after the death of Alexander Cassatt in 1906. No love was lost between his widow, Lois, and Cassatt, and this coolness affected her relationships with the children. However, her still growing circle of American friends was more enthusiastic about her work, and it was one of these, J. Howard Whittemore, who acquired the picture in 1915. Any expression of appreciation from her countrymen particularly affected her, and she wrote to Whittemore: 'It is a great pleasure and gratification to me that you like and want to own that particular picture the 'Tonda' for I have always thought it one of my best – Will you do me a favor? Take the Tonda, & keep it for sometime, if once you have it on your walls and continue to like it then I will sell it to you . . . '

As with her work for the 1892 Chicago mural, Cassatt adapted the form to her own style rather than vice versa. The circular ground has not dramatically affected the prevailing compositional mode in which she was working at the time. By 1905 she had already experimented with a three-figure group (in *The Caress*, for example) and a slightly more specific setting. What *is* unusual here is the rotation of the group away from the picture plane, so that the faces of mother and baby are hidden, and their silhouette spreads across the circle to fill it and create a strong contrast of tones diagonally. As with the Chicago mural, this project spawned various related paintings, although these were used more as experiments with colour and the use of props than to expand on the given theme.

Sleepy Baby, c. 1910

64.8 × 52.1cm, Dallas Museum of Fine Arts, Munger Fund

By 1910 Cassatt was concentrating on her pastel work, focusing on the drawing of the human figure and the expression of maternal love. She was still capable of great precision in her drawing and of a surprisingly animated use of colour. Here the shadowed areas of the mother's dress and the baby's flesh are picked out in bright blue, its electrifying effect heightened by its application in tight zigzag strokes. The colours seem almost too extreme to be faithful to the intended mood of quiet – a mother watching over her sleeping baby. *Sleepy Baby* marks a fine return to the simpler compositions on the maternity theme, with the figures presented frontally and in close-up.

Mary Cassatt

The Crochet Lesson, 1913

76.5 × 64.7cm, Private collection

The last decade of Cassatt's life was marked by frustration over her failing eyesight, which eventually ended her creative work in 1915, and by enforced separation from her extended family of household and friends, brought about by the First World War. The years immediately before the outbreak of war were anxious ones, during which she became both domestically and artistically isolated. Unsurprisingly, her last images were comforting reminders of the female grace and intimacy which had sustained her art and many of her closest friendships, but the delicacy of her subjects is overwhelmed by the strident colour, which by this late stage was no longer held in check by precision of line. Cassatt's pastels were still striking, but lacked the control of her finest works from the 1890s. Nevertheless, the artist firmly believed that these pictures were her best, the culmination of years of study and effort.

This picture represents yet again an action which signified femininity, as accepted by the society of which Cassatt was ever a part, but it is still her gift to endow the crochet lesson with a deeper sense of female relationships. The two women – sisters, or possibly a young mother and her daughter – are contained within a single silhouette, as in many of Cassatt's earlier mother and child pieces, and this closesness is made explicit by their joined hands, the parallel movement of the right arms and the single direction of their attention. As with the picture of baby John, bright pinks and blues are employed in areas of flesh and shade, and it is the colouring which threatens to distract us from the successful passages around the faces and hands, less distinct but still expressive of peaceful concentration.

Mary Cassatt

CHRONOLOGY

1844
Born Mary Stevenson Cassatt in Allegheny City, Pennsylvania (now Pittsburgh), 22nd May.
1845
Her father, Robert Simpson Cassatt, a successful banker, is elected mayor of Allegheny City.
1850–5
The family (Mr and Mrs Cassatt and their children Lydia, Alexander, Robbie, Mary and Joseph Gardner) travel in Europe, spending extended periods in Paris, Heidelberg and Darmstadt. Robbie dies in 1855.
1860–2
Attends lectures at the Pennsylvania Academy of Fine Arts in Philadelphia, but later spends her time affiliated to this institution in studies of her own.
1865–6
Travels to Paris for further training. Gains a licence to copy masterpieces in the Louvre, and briefly enrols as a pupil of Academicians Charles Chaplin and Jean Léon Gérôme.
1867–70
Studies in artists' colonies at Courances and Ecouen, near Paris, particularly with Thomas Couture, Paul Soyer and Edouard Frère, and turns to the production of genre pictures.
1868
A Mandolin Player is accepted for the Paris Salon, where it is hung 'on the line'. Moves to Villiers-le-Bel, near Ecouen, to study with Couture.
1869
Her Salon picture is rejected. Sketching trip with friend, a Miss Gordon, in the Piedmont region of Italy and France.
1870–1
Spends the summer in Rome. Is forced to return to the United States on the outbreak of the Franco-Prussian War. A frustrating period – isolated from further training and unable to sell her work. Arrives back in Europe in December 1871.
1872
Travels to Parma with fellow-student and friend Emily Sartain, to execute a copy of Correggio. Also studies the work of Parmigianino at the local academy with Carlo Raimondi. *At the Carnival* is accepted for the Paris Salon.
1872–4
Travels alone to Madrid to copy in the Prado, then moves to Seville to paint, including further successful pieces for the Salon. Returns to Paris. Travels to Antwerp with her mother to study Rubens and Hals, then back to Paris. Returns to Rome alone. Pictures are exhibited in the United States.
1874
A painting, *Ida*, is exhibited at the Salon, where it attracts Degas' praise. Works at Villiers-le-Bel in the summer, but returns to Paris in the autumn. First feels the influence of Degas' work. Meets Louisine Elder, later Mrs H. O. Havemeyer.
1875
Spends the summer in Philadelphia, but returns to settle in Paris, at 19 rue Laval.
1877
Meets Degas and is invited to participate in the exhibitions of the Independents, known as the 'Impressionists'. Her parents and Lydia arrive to settle permanently in Paris, in an apartment at 13 avenue Trudaine.
1879
Shows eleven works at the fourth Impressionist exhibition. She visits England in the summer, tours the Alps, and begins to make prints for the proposed journal *Le Jour et la nuit*.
1880
Participates in the fifth Impressionist exhibition. The household takes a country villa to accommodate the extended visit of Alexander and Lois Cassatt and their four young children, who all act as models. Produces first treatments of the maternity theme.
1881
Participates in the sixth Impressionist exhibition. Paul Durand-Ruel begins to represent her.
1882
Boycotts this year's Impressionist exhibition with Degas, after a dispute over the group's membership. Lydia dies, 7th November. Cassatt is unable to work for almost two years. In Philadelphia, Alexander resigns as Vice-President of the Pennsylvania Railroad.
1883
Travels to Spain with Mrs Cassatt, who is in poor health.
1886
Organizes and participates in the eighth (and final) Impressionist

exhibition, and shows some works at the Impressionist show organized by Durand-Ruel at his New York gallery.

1887

Moves to an apartment in the rue Marignan, which remains her Parisian residence for the rest of her life.

1888

Breaks a leg in a riding accident, which further disrupts her work.

1889–90

Exhibits at two annual exhibitions of the *Société des peintres-graveurs français*.

1890

Visits exhibition of Japanese art at the École des Beaux-Arts in Paris, and begins experimenting with colour printmaking techniques.

1891

The *Société des peintres-graveurs français* excludes Cassatt and Pissarro from its exhibition as artists of foreign birth, but the two are given adjacent exhibition space at Durand-Ruel's. Cassatt shows her 'Set of Ten' colour prints, with two pastels and two oils on the maternity theme. This constitutes her solo exhibition debut. Her father dies, 9th December.

1892

Commissioned to paint a mural on the theme of *Modern Woman* for the Women's Building of the Chicago World's Fair. Spends the summer and autumn dealing with administration, altering her studio at the rented Château Bachivillers to accommodate the huge canvas, and working on the design.

1893

Ships the finished *Modern Woman* canvas to Chicago; it receives mixed critical reviews. Has a second and major individual show, with 98 works, at Durand-Ruel's in November.

1894

Buys the Château de Beaufresne at Mesnil-Théribus, fifty miles from Paris, and begins renovating it as a summer home.

1895

First major solo show held in the United States, at Durand-Ruel's New York gallery. Her mother dies, 21st October.

1898–9

Visits family and friends in the United States.

1901

Accompanies Mr and Mrs H. O. Havemeyer on an extended tour of Spain and Italy, advising them on art purchases.

1904

Is made a Chevalier of the Légion d'honneur by the French government, one of the few honours she chooses to accept.

1906

Alexander, President of the Pennsylvania Railroad since 1899, dies, 28th December.

1908–9

Makes her last visit to the United States. A severe bout of sickness on the voyage causes her to vow never to make the journey again.

1910–11

Joins her brother Gardner and his family on a holiday in Egypt. Gardner is taken ill and dies, 5th April 1911. Devastated, Cassatt is again unable to work.

1912

Gives interviews to Achille Segard which later form the basis of her first biography, *Mary Cassatt, Un Peintre des enfants et des mères*, published the next year.

1914

Outbreak of the First World War forces her from Mesnil-Théribus and she moves to the south of France, staying at the Villa Angeletto, in Grasse. While there she visits Renoir. She is awarded the Gold Medal of Honor by the Pennsylvania Academy.

1915

Her active career ceases, due to blindness, but her work is shown at the Suffrage Loan Exhibition of Old Masters and Works by Edgar Degas and Mary Cassatt in New York. She undergoes the first of several operations for cataracts.

1917

Degas dies, and Cassatt helps deal with his estate. Their correspondence is destroyed.

1923–4

A mistake over a reprinted set of drypoint plates causes the end of her friendship with Louisine Havemeyer.

1926

Dies at the Château de Beaufresne, 14th June.

LIST OF PLATES

71: *Mrs Cassatt Reading to her Grandchildren*, 1880, oil on canvas, 55.7 × 100 cm, Private Collection.
73: *Lydia Working at a Tapestry Frame, c.* 1881, oil on canvas, 65.5 × 92 cm, Flint Institute of Arts, Michigan, Gift of the Whiting Foundation.
75: *Susan Seated Outdoors, Wearing a Purple Hat, c.* 1881, oil on canvas, 69.7 × 87.5 cm, Manoogian Collection.
77: *Portrait of a Young Woman in Black (Mrs Gardner Cassatt)*, 1883, oil on canvas, 80 × 64.1 cm, The Peabody Institute of Baltimore, on indefinite loan to The Baltimore Museum of Art.
79: *Lady at the Tea Table*, 1883–85, oil on canvas, 73.4 × 61 cm, The Metropolitan Museum of Art, New York, Gift of the Artist.
81: *Two Children at the Seashore*, 1884, watercolour, 97.6 × 74 cm, National Gallery of Art, Washington, DC.
83: *Alexander J. Cassatt and his Son, Robert Kelso Cassatt*, 1885, oil on canvas, 100 × 81.2 cm, Philadelphia Museum of Art, The W.P. Wilstach Collection and Gift of Mrs William Coxe Wright.
85: *The Sisters, c.* 1885, oil on canvas, 46.2 × 56 cm, Glasgow Art Gallery and Museum.
87: *Mr Robert S. Cassatt on Horseback*, 1885, oil on canvas, 91.5 × 71 cm, Adelson Galleries, Inc., New York.
89: *Young Woman Working in a Garden (Femme Cousant), c.* 1886, oil on canvas, 91.5 × 64.7 cm, Musée d'Orsay, Paris.
91: *Girl Arranging her Hair*, 1886, oil on canvas, 75 × 62.3 cm, National Gallery of Art, Washington, DC, Chester Dale Collection.
93: *The Letter* (fourth state), 1890–91, drypoint and aquatint, 34.5 × 21.1 cm, The Metropolitan Museum of Art, New York, Gift of Paul J. Sachs.
95: *The Dress Fitting* (seventh state), 1890–91, drypoint and aquatint, 37.7 × 25.6 cm, The Metropolitan Museum of Art, New York, Gift of Paul J. Sachs.
97: *Afternoon Tea Party* (fifth state), 1890–91, drypoint and aquatint, 34.8 × 26.3 cm, The Metropolitan Museum of Art, New York, Gift of Paul J. Sachs.
99: *Woman Bathing* (fourth state), 1890–91, drypoint and aquatint, 37.1 × 27 cm, Worcester Art Museum, Worcester, Massachusetts, Bequest of Mrs Kingsmill Marrs.
101: *In the Omnibus* (seventh state), 1890–91, drypoint and aquatint, 38.4 × 26.7 cm, Boston Public Library, Print Department.
103: *Mother's Kiss* (fifth state), 1890–91, drypoint and aquatint, 38.4 × 26.7 cm, Whittemore Collection, Library of Congress, Washington, DC.
105: *Baby's First Caress, c.* 1891, pastel on paper, 76.2 × 61.0 cm, New Britain Museum of American Art, Connecticut, Harriet Russell Stanley Memorial Fund.
107: *The Bath*, 1891–92, oil on canvas, 100.3 × 66 cm, Art Institute of Chicago, The Robert A. Waller Fund.
109: *The Family*, 1892, oil on canvas, 81.2 × 66 cm, The Chrysler Museum, Norfolk, Virginia.
111: *Gathering Fruit* (eleventh state), *c.* 1893, drypoint, soft-ground etching and aquatint, 42.2 × 29.8 cm, The Metropolitan Museum of Art, New York, Rogers Fund 1918.
113: *Baby Reaching for an Apple*, 1893, oil on canvas, 100.3 × 65.4 cm, Virginia Museum of Fine Arts, Richmond, Gift of an Anonymous Donor, 1975.
115: *In the Garden*, 1893, pastel on paper, 73 × 60 cm, The Baltimore Museum of Art, The Cone Collection, formed by Dr Claribel Cone and Miss Etta Cone of Baltimore, Maryland.
117: *The Boating Party*, 1894, oil on canvas, 90.2 × 117.1 cm, National Gallery of Art, Washington, DC, Chester Dale Collection.
119: *Summertime*, 1894, oil on canvas, 73.7 × 96.5 cm, Armand Hammer Foundation, Los Angeles, California.
121: *Portrait of Mrs H. O. Havemeyer*, 1896, pastel, 73.6 × 61 cm, Shelburne Museum, Shelburne, Vermont.
123: *The Conversation, c.* 1896, pastel on paper laid on canvas, 64.6 × 81.2 cm, Private Collection.
125: *Mother Combing Her Child's Hair*, 1898, pastel and gouache on tan paper, 64 × 80 cm, The Brooklyn Museum, Bequest of Mary T. Cockcroft.
127: *Mother and Boy (The Oval Mirror)*, 1901, oil on canvas, 81.7 × 66 cm, The Metropolitan Museum of Art, New York, Bequest of Mrs H. O. Havemeyer, 1929, The H.O. Havemeyer Collection.
129: *Young Mother Sewing*, 1902, oil on canvas, 92.3 × 73.7 cm, The Metropolitan Museum of Art, New York, Bequest of Mrs H. O. Havemeyer, 1929, The H.O. Havemeyer Collection.
131: *Margot in Blue*, 1902, pastel, 61 × 50, The Walters Art Gallery, Baltimore, Maryland.
133: *Mother and Child, c.* 1905, oil on canvas, 92.1 × 73.7 cm, National Gallery of Art, Washington, DC, Chester Dale Collection.
135: *Mother and Two Children*, 1905, oil on canvas (tondo), 100.5 cm diameter, Westmoreland County Museum of Art, Greensburg, Pennsylvania, Anonymous Gift.
137: *Sleepy Baby, c.* 1910, pastel, 64.8 × 52.1 cm, Dallas Museum of Fine Arts, Munger Fund.
139: *The Crochet Lesson*, 1913, pastel on paper, 76.5 × 64.7 cm, Private Collection.

BIBLIOGRAPHY

Only the more accessible works relating to Cassatt's life and art are given here. A more complete list of the extensive literature her career has inspired may be found in BACHMANN, Donna G. and PILAND, Sherry, *Women Artists: an historical, contemporary and feminist bibliography*, New Jersey and London, 1978.

Monographs and articles

BREESKIN, Adelyn Dohme, *Mary Cassatt: a catalogue raisonné of the oils, pastels, watercolours, and drawings*, Washington, DC, 1970.
BREESKIN, Adelyn Dohme, *A catalogue raisonné of the graphic works*, 2nd edn. Washington DC, 1979.
BUETTNER, Stuart, 'Images of modern motherhood in the art of Morisot, Cassatt, Modersohn-Becker, Kollwitz', *Woman's Art Journal*, vol. 7 Fall/Winter 1986/7.
FILLIN-YEH, Susan, 'Mary Cassatt's images of women', *Art Journal*, vol. 35, Summer 1976.
HALE, Nancy, *Mary Cassatt*, New York, 1975.
HAVEMEYER, Louisine, 'Mary Cassatt', *The Pensylvania Museum Bulletin*, vol. 21, no.113, 1927.
KYSELA, John D., 'Mary Cassatt's mystery mural for the World's Fair of 1893', *Art Quarterly* vol. 19, 1966.
MATTHEWS, Nancy Mowll, (ed.), *Cassatt and her Circle: Selected letters*, New York, 1984.
MATHEWS, Nancy Mowll, *Mary Cassatt*, New York, 1987.
POLLOCK, Griselda, *Mary Cassatt*, London, 1980.
ROUDEBUSH, Jay, *Mary Cassatt*, Naefels, Switzerland, 1979.
SWEET, Frederick, *Miss Mary Cassatt, Impressionist from Pennsylvania*, Norman, Oklahoma, 1966.

General works

CHADWICK, Whitney, *Women, Art and Society*, London, 1990.
GARB, Tamar, *Women Impressionists*, Oxford, 1986.
HOOPES, Donelson F., *The American Impressionists*, New York, 1972.
HUYSMANS, Joris-Karl, *L'Art moderne*, Paris, 1883.
POLLOCK, Griselda, *Vision and Difference: Femininity, Feminism and the Histories of Art*, London 1988.
WHITFORD, Frank, *Japanese Prints and Western Painters*, London, 1977.

Exhibition catalogues

Major exhibitions held during the artist's lifetime are mentioned in the chronology. The following list represents a selection of the most recent.

BREESKIN, Adelyn Dohme, *Mary Cassatt 1844–1926*, National Gallery of Art, Washington, DC, 1970.
BREESKIN, Adelyn Dohme, *Paintings, Drawings and Graphic Works by Monet, Degas, Berthe Morisot and Mary Cassatt*, Baltimore Museum of Art, 1962.
BREESKIN, Adelyn Dohme, *Graphic Art of Mary Cassatt*, Museum of Graphic Art, New York, 1966.
LINDSAY, Susan G., *Mary Cassatt and Philadelphia*, Philadelphia Museum of Art, 1985.
MATHEWS, Nancy Mowll, *Mary Cassatt and Edgar Degas*, San Jose Museum of Art, California, 1982.
MATHEWS, Nancy Mowll, and SHAPIRO, Barbara Stern, *Mary Cassatt: the colour prints*, Williams College Museum of Art, Williamstown, Massachusetts, 1989.
MILKOVITCH, Michael, et al., *Mary Cassatt and the American Impressionists*, Dixon Gallery and Gardens, Memphis, 1976.
SHAPIRO, Barbara Stern, *Mary Cassatt at Home*, Museum of Fine Arts, Boston, 1978.
SWEET, Frederick, *Sargent, Whistler and Mary Cassatt*, Art Institute of Chicago, 1954.

PHOTOGRAPH CREDITS

All photographs in this book were supplied by the owners of the works, with the following exceptions:
Scala: 10; The Chicago Historical Society: 33, 34; Bulloz: 37, 49, 63; Bridgeman Art Library: 57; Coe Kerr Gallery: 71; Réunion des Musées Nationaux: 89; Christie's, New York: 123.